THE FRUIT OF THE SPIRIT

PERMISSIONS

Appreciation is expressed to the following authors and publishers for permission to quote from their publications:

Page 26: David Ireland with Louis Thrap, *Letters to an Unborn Child* (New York: Harper & Row, 1974). Used by permission of Harper Collins Publishers.

Pages 27–29: David Wilkerson, "Keep Yourself in the Love of God," *Times Square Church Pulpit Series*, World Challenge, Inc., P.O. Box 260, Lindale, TX 75771 (25 October 1999). Used by permission.

Pages 30–81: Joseph Stowell, *Loving Those We'd Rather Hate* (Chicago: Moody Press, 1994), as adapted for "God's Compassion for Sinners," in *Preaching Today* (Carol Stream, IL: Leadership Resources and Christianity Today, Inc.).

Page 129: Max Lucado, *When God Whispers Your Name* (Dallas; Word, 1994). All rights reserved.

THE FRUIT OF THE SPIRIT

Becoming the Person God Wants You to Be

THOMAS E. TRASK &
WAYDE I. GOODALL

EMANATE

BOOKS

Published in Nashville, Tennessee, by Emanate Books, an imprint of Thomas Nelson. Emanate Books and Thomas Nelson are registered trademarks of HarperCollins Christian Publishing, Inc.

Thomas Nelson titles may be purchased in bulk for educational, business, fund-raising, or sales promotional use. For information, please e-mail SpecialMarkets@ ThomasNelson.com.

Any Internet addresses, phone numbers, or company or product information printed in this book are offered as a resource and are not intended in any way to be or to imply an endorsement by Thomas Nelson, nor does Thomas Nelson vouch for the existence, content, or services of these sites, phone numbers, companies, or products beyond the life of this book.

Also published in Spanish by Vida Publishers, ISBN 0-829-73200-4.

ISBN 978-1-4002-0914-9 (TP)

Library of Congress Cataloging-in-Publication Data

Trask, Thomas E.
The Fruit of the Spirit: becoming the person God wants you to be / Thomas E. Trask and Wayde I. Goodall.
p. cm.
Includes bibliographical references and index.
ISBN 0-310-22787-9 (softcover)
1. Fruit of the Spirit. I. Goodall, Wayde I. II.Title.
BV4501.2 .T685 2000
234'13.—dc21   00-028973

Printed in the United States of America
18 19 20 21 22 LSC 10 9 8 7 6 5 4 3 2 1

CONTENTS

CONTENTS

FOREWORD

I am thrilled that my dear friend Thomas E. Trask and Wayde Goodall have written this outstanding book about the fruit of the Spirit, a greatly needed emphasis in the body of Christ today. I strongly recommend this book for both individual and group study.

When you think about it, there can be nothing more important to us and to the world than the fruit of the Holy Spirit. Hurting humanity desperately needs that which comes from God: his love, his joy, his peace, and all the other wonderful manifestations of his Spirit.

In the mystery of the Trinity, the fruit of the Spirit is really the life of our Lord Jesus Christ. It is his Spirit, whom the Father sent. As his Spirit indwells and controls us, his fruit, or personality, becomes manifest as we yield ourselves to him.

For many years I have taught the absolute necessity of being filled with and controlled by the Holy Spirit. This has been a cornerstone teaching of the entire Campus Crusade for Christ movement, which now has more than 21,000 full-time staff and almost 500,000 trained volunteers in 184 countries. It is only as we are filled with the Holy Spirit and under his control that his fruit is manifest and his will expressed, such as helping to fulfill the Great Commission, the task to which all believers are called.

Sharing Christ and his message of love and forgiveness is the result of his fruit of love and compassion flowing through us.

There are two wonderful secrets that have changed my life and that of many others. The first is how we are filled with the Holy Spirit by faith, according to God's command (Eph. 5:18) and his promise (1 John 5:14–15). We ask, believe, and receive. The second is how the fruit of the Holy Spirit is demonstrated through us by faith. For example, we can actually love people by faith on the basis of God's command and promise. Even those who may appear unlovable and even if we do not feel like it, our Lord wants to love, through us, the way he loves us, even though by his standards none of us are lovable. This fruit of the Spirit working through millions of believers by faith could literally change the world.

With great God-given skill and from many years of walking with the Lord, Dr. Trask and Dr. Goodall have masterfully given us this marvelous book about the precious fruit of the Spirit. I pray that the inspired contents of this book will richly bless and even change the life of all readers and the world around them.

This is must reading for every sincere believer!

Dr. Bill Bright
Founder and President,
Campus Crusade for Christ International

INTRODUCTION

When my family and I (Wayde) were missionaries in Vienna, Austria, we lived in a quaint village called Grinzing on the edge of the Vienna woods on the outskirts of Vienna. Grinzing is surrounded by flowing hills lined with meticulous rows of vineyards, and a certain path through the vineyards is called the "Beethoven Path," because tradition tells us that it was the composer's favorite place to walk. For part of his life Beethoven lived in a flat at Grinzinger Strasse 64 where he wrote his Symphony no. 6, "Pastoral."[1] Beethoven may have gazed from his apartment window at his peaceful pastoral surroundings and been inspired to write this symphony.

When I lived in Grinzing I often watched the vineyard farmers from the hilltops where I went to pray. Each fall, as a result of their hard work the rest of the year, the grape farmers would bring in the harvest. After the harvest they would prune the vines to near ground level. The first time I watched them I thought they were going to destroy their vines. During the winter months all I could see on the hills were rows of stakes holding up wire. I couldn't imagine how the farmers could hope to produce a profitable crop the next season. Yet each farmer carefully tilled the soil and checked the wire lines and stakes to be sure they were firmly connected to each other. The farmers seemed sure that they were doing the right thing and that the fall would see a good harvest. The cold winter soon transitioned into spring, and as the trees of Vienna began to blossom, the vineyards began to produce vines that quickly grew up the stakes and across the wires, and soon tiny grapes appeared that would ripen for the fall harvest.

The farmers really did know what they were doing! Until I had watched an entire growing cycle, I did not understand why the farmers did what they did. Each pruned the branches drastically and tilled the soil faithfully even when there was no evidence that the branches would produce a good harvest. They knew from past experience that if they did their job effectively and the weather cooperated, they would witness a tremendous harvest.

When Jesus was explaining to his disciples how they would be able to produce God's fruit, he used the analogy of a vineyard (see John 15:1–17). He said they were like the branches of a vine the heavenly Father, the Gardener, would prune so that they could produce fruit. He also told them what the fruit would look like and why some branches had to be destroyed. Jesus Christ, the Vine, is perfect. He desires for us to produce fruit like that of our Creator, and he knows that this is possible only if we are connected to him. As we grow in our Christian walk, we understand more and more why we must be pruned.

HOW CAN WE PRODUCE GOD'S FRUIT?

Pastor and author Stuart Briscoe tells the story of a friend who often used an old fruit tree to escape from his second-story bedroom window, especially when his father was about to punish him. One day the father announced that he was going to cut down the old tree because it had not borne fruit in many years. That night the boy and his friends purchased a bushel of apples and in the cover of darkness tied fruit to the unproductive branches. The next morning the father shouted to his wife, "Mary, I can't believe my eyes. The old fruit tree that was barren for years is covered with apples. It's a miracle because it's a pear tree!"[2]

As any vineyard or orchard owner knows, dried up, dead branches do not produce fruit, for the branches are unable to receive nourishment from the vine. If the branches are healthy and properly connected to the vine, however, so that nutrients can flow through them, they will produce fruit as healthy as the vine to which they are attached. Likewise, we will produce the kind of fruit that pleases God if we are connected to his Son. Jesus said, "I am the vine; you are the branches" (John 15:5). When our lives are totally committed to God and we are determined to obey him, we will bear the fruit of Christ because he is the Vine! We cannot help bearing all the fruit of the Spirit when we *remain* in him. Neil Anderson, in his book *Daily in Christ*, explains:

> The soul of the spiritual person reflects a change generated by spiritual birth. He can now receive his impetus from the Spirit, not just from the flesh. His mind is being renewed and transformed. Peace and joy instead of turmoil characterize his emotions. It is our responsibility to choose not to walk according to the flesh, but to walk according to the Spirit. As the spiritual person exercises his choice to live in the Spirit, his life bears the fruit of the Spirit.[3]

This truth could be seen in the life of the great professional golfer Payne Stewart. The sports world was shocked when, in a tragic and bizarre plane crash, Stewart's life was suddenly taken in the fall of 1999. Golfers everywhere were talking about his performance that year as the world watched him come back from a loss in the 1998 U.S. Open to win in 1999 by holing a fifteen-foot putt on the final hole. He also played a key role in the Ryder Cup victory.

Not only were professional golfers respectful of Stewart's ability on the course, but they were even more amazed by his changed life. The man who had once been restless and uncaring about what the press or public thought of him had experienced a dramatic change. None of Stewart's friends can pinpoint the exact moment of his conversion, but his pastor, J. B. Collingsworth of Orlando, said, "People have prayed for a long time. I told him, 'With you, it will probably happen in a hotel room.' With him, it almost crept up on him."[4]

Though Stewart made a private decision to surrender his life to Christ, the public most definitely noticed the change Stewart's sister described in his preconversion behavior: "He got irritated with the press. He didn't like some of the questions they'd ask and he'd be kind of rude. Sometimes he was churlish in public."[5] Of Stewart's postconversion lifestyle, a friend said, "I think he became more settled; he could focus, then overcome adversity. When he got a bad shot, he could go up and approach it and play smart golf."[6] Jim Morris, sixty-eight, who had become a surrogate father to Stewart, said he was proud of what Payne had become before his death. He summed up the change in Payne's life by saying that the boy turned man had set priorities: faith first, family second, himself third.[7]

In Springfield, Missouri, the city where Stewart had grown up, the local newspaper reported,

Most everyone who knew or followed Payne Stewart noticed a difference in him the year before his death: The 42-year-old golfer who had once snapped at autograph seekers, berated reporters and pulled a few not-so-tasteful pranks had, it appeared, grown up.

At first, it was hard to know where Stewart's newfound peace came from. Some credit Stewart's wife, Tracey, who urged him to attend a public relations class to help his image. Others say Payne was simply growing up, placing increased importance on the things of adulthood—his church, family, and vocation.

But the WWJD (What Would Jesus Do) bracelet on Stewart's wrist became the telltale sign for almost everyone. Stewart had returned to the religious faith he learned about as a child, and everything else had fallen neatly into place.[8]

I am sure Payne Stewart looked for joy and peace in a lot of places. He probably was frustrated by his lack of self-control with the public, and inside he wanted to be kind to people in general. But his personal stamina didn't work. He changed when he made the decision to give Jesus Christ total control of his life. One of his friends said, "There was a calm about him you only find in someone who has found what life and joy are all about."[9]

The Vine

Jesus said in John 15:1, "I am the true (*alethinos*) vine" (John 15:1). He could have said, "I am *a* vine" or "I am *the* vine," but he wanted to emphatically communicate to his disciples that he is the only vine that is legitimate. The meaning of the original word *alethinos* is "true, real, genuine." Jesus is truth; and he is the only vine that branches can be connected to in order to produce God's fruit. He is the Creator; the sinless, omnipotent Son of God; and the only way to heaven. He speaks with authority as no one else can.

Andrew Murray said,

> The connection between a vine and a branch is a living one.
> No work of a human can effect it; the branch is such only
> by the Creator's own work, in virtue of which the life and
> the fruitfulness of the vine communicate themselves to the
> branch.
>
> And so it is with believers. The believer's union with the
> Lord Jesus is no work of human wisdom or of human will,
> but an act of God by which the closest and the most complete
> life-union is effected between the Son of God and the sinner:
> "God hath sent forth the Spirit of his Son into your hearts"
> (Gal. 4:6 KJV). The same Spirit who dwelt, and still dwells, in
> the Son becomes the life of the believer; in the unity of that one
> Spirit and the fellowship of the same life which is in Christ, the
> believer is one with him. Just as between a vine and a branch,
> the union between the Vine and the believer is a life-union that
> makes them one.
>
> Without the Vine the branch can do nothing. To the
> Vine it owes its right of place in the vineyard, its life and its
> fruitfulness.[10]

As a follower of Jesus Christ, you are connected to the Vine.
Through his roots, the nourishment of the Spirit flows into you
and enables you to act like Christ and exhibit "the fruit of the
Spirit." You are different from what you were before you gave
your life to Christ. Before, you could not have modeled the kind
of love, peace, self-control, or kindness that is the Spirit's fruit.
But when you daily cling to and rely on the Vine, you will grow
God's fruit, for this is a supernatural ability that only believers
in Christ can enjoy. Loving people who are not Christians have
shown tremendous acts of kindness. If, however, they had been

connected to the Vine, think how much more they could have been and done.

The Gardener

Jesus said, "My Father is the gardener. He cuts off every branch in me that bears no fruit, while every branch that does bear fruit he prunes so that it will be even more fruitful" (John 15:1–2).

A gardener puts seed into the ground and carefully cultivates it. As the plant begins to grow branches, the gardener prunes them so that the plant will produce more fruit. Pruning strengthens a plant by ridding it of unproductive branches, and nearly all fruit plants have to be pruned at least once annually in order to produce a good crop. A farmer knows that some branches will never produce fruit and therefore cuts them off completely.

Some Christians live in fear that God will cut them off because they continue to struggle with wrong attitudes or seem continually to be tempted to do things that they know are sinful. The key for them is not to quit the faith but to remain and know that God will help them overcome. Jesus said that the will of his Father is "that I shall lose none of all that he has given me, but raise them up at the last day" (John 6:39). Though you may feel that God has been pruning you and perhaps has cut you off, you need to know that his will is that none will be lost. Discipline can be difficult and painful, but when we have been trained by it we are grateful for the lessons we have learned.

Branches that do not bear any fruit are cut off. Jesus said that we will know his disciples by the fruit they yield (see Matt. 7:15–23). Some people call themselves disciples but produce no fruit to indicate it. These people are illegitimate branches—they profess to be Christians but have words without actions, branches with leaves but no fruit. They are apostates who heard the gospel and believed it but decided not to follow the teachings of Jesus Christ. In this way they became traitors to the Lord. As humans we sometimes may have difficulty determining exactly who is a true disciple, but God always knows those who belong to him and those who do not. Fruitless branches are on their way to destruction.

We are not destroyed when we are pruned, for our heavenly Father prunes us according to his tremendous wisdom and love. If he did not prune us, we would not grow. As we mature in Christ we should even look forward to our Father's pruning and shaping, for he sees things in our lives that we do not see. He knows our hearts when we do not. He has complete understanding, knows the direction we are headed, and can from his motivation of love create roadblocks in our lives. He always knows what is best for us and never intends to bring harm; rather, he will help us become more like his Son.

God typically prunes his children by conviction from the Holy Spirit; when we contemplate sinning he convicts us for our feelings, thinking, or behavior. Conviction makes us feel guilty and motivates us to stop what we are doing that is displeasing to God. All of us struggle with sin in our lives, and thus we also experience conviction. The Holy Spirit is our trusted friend who warns us to flee temptation and shows us what we need to do to avoid living an unholy life. What a wonderful blessing it is to know that God is watching out for us in case our motives are wrong or our plans are potentially harmful to us. We need to listen to his loving conviction.

Ravi Zacharias wrote in his book *Deliver Us from Evil,*

It is imperative that the Christian learn to differentiate in his or her own beliefs between opinion and conviction. An opinion is merely a preference in a continuum of options. A person may prefer one color to another or one style to another. A conviction, on the other hand, is rooted in the conscience and cannot be changed without changing that which essentially defines the person. In a pluralistic culture, an opinion should not be given the same passion as the weight of a conviction. And every conviction held must be done so with the clear and required teaching of Scripture. Once these differences are made in a Christian's mind then a very important logical consequence follows: Every conviction that is held should be undergirded by love.[11]

Another way that God typically prunes his children is by discipline. The writer of Hebrews tells us, "Endure hardship as discipline; God is treating you as sons. For what son is not disciplined by his father? If you are not disciplined (and everyone undergoes discipline), then you are illegitimate children and not true sons. . . . God disciplines us for our good, that we may share in his holiness" (Heb. 12:7–8, 10).

In the 1990s many owners of small farms in America began to reduce their wholesale farming to a mere sideline and started using their property for another purpose: entertainment farming, also known as *agritainment* and *agritourism*. Entertainment farmers attract paying customers to their property with country bands, hay-bale or cornfield mazes, petting corrals, and tricycle courses. City-dwelling families eager for a feel of life on the farm pay for admission, food, and amusements.

Sometimes a Christian or a church is diverted from the central purpose of producing fruit and resembles an entertainment farmer instead. But fruitfulness is God's will for every Christian and every church. When we are fruitless we can be assured that we have turned aside from our purpose and God will bring conviction and/or discipline.

God cares about us and will discipline us so that we can be participants in his holiness, righteousness, and peace. Some of us may remember the saying; "I'll need to take him to the woodshed." This was the place where discipline took place, where Mom or Dad carried out the difficult task of helping a child understand that his or her behavior was unacceptable. On the wall of one woodshed hung a belt with the inscription above it, "I need thee every hour!" Likewise, if we are to become better persons, we need God's loving discipline. Since God's discipline—our being pruned—makes us holier and in turn produces more fruit, we should desire his discipline.

The Branches

Jesus tells us, "I am the vine; you are the branches. If a man remains in me and I in him, he will bear much fruit; apart from me you can do nothing" (John 15:5).

The word *remain* is used ten times in the first ten verses of John 15. As Christians we are branches, and to produce fruit we must "remain" in the Vine. William Barclay explains,

> Suppose a person is weak. He has fallen into temptation; he has made a mess of things; he is on the way down to degeneracy of mind and heart and mental fiber. Now suppose that he has a friend of a strong and lovely and loving nature, who rescues him from his degraded situation. There is only one way in which he can retain his reformation and keep himself on the right way. He must keep contact with his friend. If he loses that contact, all the chances are that his weakness will overcome him; the old temptations will rear their heads again; and he will fall. His salvation lies in continual contact with the strength of his friend.[12]

Some of us know that we need to be in relationship with certain healthy people because they encourage us, counsel us, and give us strength. We know that as long as they are around we are safe. I have watched people who come from devastating pasts, including lives of abuse and addiction to drugs, alcohol, or gambling. When they determine to trust Christ and grow in the faith, they are safe. Some of them decide along the way to return to some of their old ways. They begin to miss church services, avoid some of their strong Christian friends, associate with their previous non-Christian friends, and rationalize that they are strong enough to do some of what they did when their lives were a mess. They subtly slip back into the black hole of devastation. They do not remain in the victory of the Lord and the enemy of their souls is ready to snatch them back.

We must hunger desperately for ways to cling to the Vine, our life source. Our lives must constantly demonstrate our desire to hold onto Jesus, to cling to him, and to become like him. We can be assured that if we remain in the Lord he will produce through us fruit that reminds people of him.

The *Leadership Bible* gives excellent insight into this truth.

> Jesus often used nature to illustrate spiritual truth, and the organic metaphor in this passage speaks of reproductive life. The vine, branches, and fruit constitute an integrated biological system in which the fruit is derived from the nutrients of the soil. Just as the branch must receive its life from the vine, so believers must depend upon and look to the life of Christ within them to find their spiritual vitality. And just as the fruit nourishes others and contains within itself the seeds of its own reproduction, so the outward manifestation of the life of Christ in us nourishes and reproduces his life in others. If any part of the system malfunctions, the byproduct of the fruit will fail to appear.[13]

The secret to Jesus' fruitful life was his contact with the Father. Luke informs us that "Jesus often withdrew to lonely places and prayed" (Luke 5:16). We too must keep in contact with—that is, remain in—Jesus by praying, reading our Bibles, and obeying what we read. Our remaining in Christ is the key to our survival. Therefore, every day we must deliberately make an effort to find ways to communicate with him, depend on him, and obey what he tells us to do. We sincerely want God's direction and advice and the true wisdom that can come only from him.

God also provides our spiritual nourishment. At times our daily devotional life makes us feel incredibly close to God, but much of the time it is something like eating a meal. We "feel" little if anything spiritual other than that we are seeking a closer relationship with Christ. However, when we have communicated with the "Truth" and have been in his presence, the desire to touch anything evil is diminished.

The Fruit

Jesus tells us that it is for the "Father's glory, that you bear much fruit, showing yourselves to be my disciples" (John 15:8). Billy Graham comments on the difference between "fruits" and "fruit": "It is interesting that the Bible talks of the fruit of the Spirit rather than the fruits. A tree may bear many apples, but all come from the same tree. In the same way, the Holy Spirit is the source of all fruit in our lives."[14] As our life is enriched by Christ we demonstrate many Christlike attributes and bring glory to God. In Martin Luther's commentary on Galatians, he said that those who follow the Lord "bring with them most excellent fruits and maximum usefulness, for they that have them give glory to God, and with the same do allure and provoke others to embrace the doctrine and faith of Christ."[15]

When people experience our fruit by seeing us act in ways that are different from the ways the world would act, they want to know more about the God who enabled us to be this way. In his book *The Fruit of the Spirit*, Manford George Gutzke compares the fruit of the Spirit to beams of light: "All the colors of the rainbow are in every beam of sunlight. They are all there at any one time. They may not always come into vision, but they are all present. It is not necessary to think of them as being so many separate colors. Just as these colors of the rainbow are present in light, so these traits of personal conduct are in the working of the Holy Spirit."[16] All the fruit is available whenever we need that particular type, whether it is patience with a boss or a child or kindness toward someone who is helpless to return the favor. God is glorified when we show others by the fruit we display that we are disciples of Jesus.

The fruit that Jesus' disciples display is different from the fruit of those who only appear to be connected to the Vine. Although they may look legitimate, their actions prove they are not. John tells us that "those who obey his commands live in him, and he in them. And this is how we know that he lives in us: We know it by the Spirit he gave us" (1 John 3:24). Again John instructs us, "If anyone obeys his word, God's love is truly made complete in him. This is how we know we are in him" (1 John 2:5). Our obedience to Christ's commands proves that we remain in him. If we disobey him and his Word, we will not bear his fruit, for we will have chosen to *disconnect* and not *remain*. This is a sobering thought. If we choose not to live a life in Christ that will bring glory to him and to live a life of disobedience instead, we can anticipate God's judgment. Jesus said that such a person is "like a branch that is thrown away and withers; such branches are picked up, thrown into the fire and burned" (John 15:6).

Missionary John Hess Yoder provides a comparison from culture that shows the difference between those who bear Christ's fruit and those who choose to disobey God's ways.

While serving as a missionary in Laos, I discovered an illustration of the kingdom of God.

Before the colonialists imposed national boundaries, the

kings of Laos and Vietnam reached an agreement on taxation in the border areas. Those who ate short-grain rice, built their houses on stilts, and decorated them with Indian-style serpents were considered Laotians. On the other hand, those who ate long-grain rice, built their houses on the ground, and decorated them with Chinese-style dragons were considered Vietnamese.

The exact location of a person's home was not what determined his or her nationality. Instead, each person belonged to the kingdom whose cultural values he or she exhibited.[17]

Likewise, Christians live in the world but, as citizens of God's kingdom, display his values.

Peter H. Davids, in his commentary on 1 Peter, defines the world as "human culture in its independence of and hostility toward God."[18] Instead of acting like those who belong to this world, we are to demonstrate the fruit of God's Spirit by cooperating with him through our dependence on him.

WHAT DOES GOD'S FRUIT LOOK LIKE?

People Fruit

People fruit consists of people we have introduced to Christ or influenced in a positive way for him. The apostle Paul wrote to the Roman Christians, "I planned many times to come to you . . . in order that I might have a harvest among you, just as I have had among the other Gentiles." When we walk with Christ, our life will cause others to wonder what we have. Many will be drawn to Jesus because of the positive impact he is having on our life work, and they will want what we have.

Giving Fruit

The time, energy, and money we give to the cause of Christ are fruit that help spread the gospel and minister to people in need. Paul informed the Roman believers that churches in Macedonia and Achaia made a "contribution for the poor among the saints in Jerusalem. . . . For if the Gentiles have shared in the Jews' spiritual blessings, they owe it to the Jews to share with them their material blessings" (Rom. 15:26–27). He added that he would insure that they "received this fruit" (v. 28).

Gospel Fruit

When believers spread the gospel of Christ, it will bear fruit. Paul told the Colossian believers, "All over the world this gospel is bearing fruit and growing" (Col. 1:6).

The Fruit of Praise

Praising God and telling others that Christ is Lord is fruit that honors God. The author of Hebrews instructed his readers, "Let us continually offer to God a sacrifice of praise—the fruit of lips that confess his name" (Heb. 13:15).

The Fruit of the Spirit

"The fruit of the Spirit is love, joy, peace, patience, kindness, goodness, faithfulness, gentleness and self-control" (Gal. 5:22). This book is about producing the fruit of the Spirit, the very fruit that comes from God himself. We cannot produce it on our own; however, by remaining in Jesus we will most certainly begin to yield a harvest of actions and attitudes that demonstrate we are connected to the true Vine. As we look at the nine elements of the fruit of the Holy Spirit, we would like you to consider several questions.

- When you know what is best for others, do you communicate it with compassion and love? Truth is communicated to others in an attitude of love (Eph. 4:15).
- Do you love others with actions and truth? Truth is manifested in the way we act toward others (1 John 3:18).
- Are you free from the habits of sinful actions, thoughts, and feelings? Truth sets people free from sin and bondage (John 8:32).
- Have you determined to obey the Holy Spirit every day and seek his guidance? The Holy Spirit guides believers into truth (John 16:13).
- Do you love (even crave) the truth? Truth is something that you must love (2 Thess. 2:10).
- Are you committed to being obedient when you understand what God wants you to do? Truth is something you must obey when you discover it (Gal. 5:7).
- Do you live out the truth? Truth is to be displayed (lived out) in our lives (2 Cor. 4:2). When we live in the truth, it is obvious that we are different from the world. People see that there must be something more in our lives than self-discipline, hard work, or self-control. God helps us live the way we live (John 3:21).

You may feel that you can't follow the Lord wholeheartedly. The fruit of God's Spirit is something you may be able to display on rare occasions; however, as a lifestyle it is an impossibility. You're right! You cannot consistently display the fruit of the Spirit unless you have totally surrendered your life to Jesus Christ. Because of your self-discipline, you may be able to perform random acts of love and kindness or have some sense of peace or patience; however, such acts will be inconsistent because they do not flow from the consistent flow of the Holy Spirit's power within you. And when really put to the test, perhaps in a time of trial, you may not be able to muster these virtues in your own power. That is why you must be connected to the one who supplies all the necessary ingredients for you to manifest his fruit. Billy Graham said, "The Bible tells us we need the Spirit to bring fruit into our lives because we cannot produce godliness apart from the Spirit. In our own selves we are filled with all kinds of self-centered and self-seeking desires which are opposed to God's will for our lives. In other words, two things need to happen in our lives. First, the sin in our lives needs to be thrust out. Second, the Holy Spirit needs to come in and fill our lives, producing the fruit of the Spirit."[19]

For years Augustine was a hopeless sinner torn between conflicting wills and weighed down by destructive habits. He lived a life apart from God's ways and was miserable because of it. He wrote,

> I probed the hidden depths of my soul and wrung its pitiful secrets from it, and when I mustered them all before the eyes of my heart, a great storm broke within me. Somehow I flung myself down beneath a fig tree and gave way to the tears, which now streamed from my eyes. For I felt that I was still the captive of my sins, and in misery I kept crying, "How long shall I go on saying, 'Tomorrow, tomorrow'? Why not now? Why not make an end of my ugly sins at this moment?"
>
> I was asking myself these questions, weeping all the while with the most bitter sorrow in my heart, when all at once I heard the singing of a child in a nearby house. Whether it was the voice of a boy or girl I cannot say, but again and again it repeated the refrain, "Take it and read, take it and read." At this I looked up, thinking hard whether there was any kind of game in which children used to chant words like these, but I could not remember ever hearing them before.

I stemmed my flood of tears and stood up, telling myself that this could only be a divine command to open my book of Scripture and read the first passage on which my eyes should fall. So I hurried back to the place where I had put down the book containing Paul's epistles. I seized it and opened it, and in silence I read the first passage on which my eyes fell; "Let us behave decently, as in the daytime, not in orgies and drunkenness, not in sexual immorality and debauchery, not in dissension and jealousy. Rather, clothe yourselves with the Lord Jesus Christ, and do not think about how to gratify the desires of the sinful nature" (Rom. 13:13–14).

I had no wish to read more and no need to do so. For in an instant, as I came to the end of the sentence, it was as though the light of confidence flooded into my heart and all the darkness of doubt was dispelled. I marked the place with my finger and closed the book. You converted me to yourself so that I no longer placed any hope in this world but stood firmly upon the rule of faith.[20]

Augustine discovered how to become connected to the Vine, and he determined that he would remain there for life. His life was changed. He began displaying God's fruit, and as a result the world has greatly benefited and God has been glorified. You too can display God's fruit. His love, joy, peace, patience, kindness, goodness, faithfulness, gentleness, and self-control can be part of your life.

CHAPTER 1

LOVE

Building Healthy Relationships

While doing premarital counseling in our church, I asked one young, optimistic couple, "What vows do you intend to say to one another in the ceremony?" As a pastor I had sometimes permitted couples to write their own vows if they were vows of commitment and honored God's standards for marriage. They said, "We have only adjusted the traditional marriage vows to be a little more contemporary. Let us read them to you."

Their vows seemed fine until they got to the final line of commitment: "For richer or poorer; in sickness and in health; until we no longer love each other."

I said, "Hold it. What do you mean, 'Until we no longer love each other'?" They said, "Well, couples sometimes fall out of love, and they should not be required to remain married and unhappy for the rest of their lives. Everyone has the right to be happy."

At first I was surprised, but then I thought about it and realized that society had subtly gotten to them; the lack of commitment had become part of their thinking—even on what probably would be the second most critical decision of their lives (the first being their commitment to Christ). Obviously, I needed to continue the premarital counseling sessions to explain God's plan for lifelong loving and commitment.

In *Letters to an Unborn Child*, David Ireland wrote to the child in his wife's womb partly because he knew that he may never see the child. While his wife's pregnancy developed, David was dying of a crippling neurological disease. He wrote in one of his letters,

> Your mother is very special. Few men know what it's like to receive appreciation for taking their wives out to dinner when it entails what it does for us. It means that she has to dress me, shave me, brush my teeth, comb my hair, wheel me out of the house and down the steps, open the garage and put me in the car, take the pedals off the chair, stand me up, sit me in the seat of the car, twist me around so that I'm comfortable, fold the wheelchair, put it in the car, go around to the other side of the car, start it up, back it out, get out of the car, pull the garage door down, get back into the car, and drive off to the restaurant.
>
> And then, it starts all over again; she gets out of the car, unfolds the wheelchair, opens the door, spins me around, stands me up, seats me in the wheelchair, pushes the pedals out, closes and locks the car, wheels me into the restaurant, then takes the pedals off the wheelchair so I won't be uncomfortable. We sit down to have dinner, and she feeds me throughout the entire meal. And when it's over she pays the bill, pushes the wheelchair out to the car again, and reverses the same routine.
>
> And when it's over—finished—with real warmth she'll say, "Honey, thank you for taking me out to dinner." I never quite know what to answer.[1]

What an example of courageous giving and self-sacrificing love David's wife, Joyce, provides us. She clearly understands and lives out love.

The Bible tells us that "God is love" (1 John 4:16). Thus it is no surprise that the first aspect of the fruit of the Spirit that is mentioned is love. For humans, perhaps, there is no greater power in this world than to "act" in God's love. Billy Graham has said, "Indeed, we may say that love for others is the first sign that we have been born again and that the Holy Spirit is at work in our lives."[2]

In Christ we are connected to the greatest love, the absolute source of pure, unadulterated love. If we walk in fellowship with him, we cannot help but be reminded of how to love people with our words, deeds, and actions. In fact, without Christ it is impossible to love people this way. Christlike love is called *agape* love. It is a giving, self-sacrificing love that has its source in Christ's self-giving love (see 1 Cor. 13:13). John said, "This is how we know what love is: Jesus Christ laid down his life for us. And we ought to lay down our lives for our brothers" (1 John 3:16).

We must strive to continually practice *agape* love. When we *remain* on the vine, we realize that we *should* love people with God's love. We will also be aware of ways we *could* love people. In the end, however, we will need to make the decision to *do* acts of love, for we are not robots that are given the command to love people. We are people of free will who constantly make decisions to do the right thing. The self-control (discipline) portion of the fruit of the Spirit is at work as we choose to respond to others with God's *agape* love.

CHRISTIANITY IS ABOUT RELATIONSHIPS

Jesus said, "As the Father has loved me, so have I loved you. Now remain in my love. If you obey my commands, you will remain in my love, just as I have obeyed my Father's commands and remain in his love. . . . My command is this: Love each other as I have loved you" (John 15:9–10, 12). Our relationship with God, with other Christians, and with our "neighbors" is where the reality of our Christianity is lived out. Because we have a one-on-one, personal relationship with Jesus Christ, we grow in our sensitivity to people's needs and as a result see them through the eyes of God's love. His love persuades us to take risks for the sake of others.

David Wilkerson was the founder of Teen Challenge and the pastor of Times Square Church in New York City. For decades he created new programs to reach people whom many have given up on. He wrote,

> Thirty-five years ago, God put it on my heart to start a boys' home in Amityville, New York, on Long Island. I truly sensed the Lord was behind this work. Yet, after just a year and a half, state officials put impossibly stringent regulations on the home. They told us we had to have a full-time psychologist on staff, as well as a priest or rabbi if we took in boys who were Catholic or Jewish. We couldn't afford to operate under those restrictions, so we simply shut our doors.
>
> We'd taken in only four boys during the brief time we were open, and after we closed down, I lost touch with them. I've always thought that venture was one of the greatest failures of all time. For more than three decades, I wondered why God ever allowed us to move forward with it. This past week, however, I received a letter from a man named Clifford. He told the following story:
>
>> Brother David,
>>
>> I was one of the four boys sent to your Amityville home thirty-five years ago by the Nassau County Children's Agency.
>>
>> My father and mother were Jewish, but they split up and

my mother remarried. She was such a rebel that she put me in a Catholic school. I was sprinkled in the Catholic Church when I was eleven years old.

Right after that, our home became dysfunctional. I had to clean the whole house, cook, take care of my little brother, and care for my mom while working a paper route early in the morning. Once I had to break into my mother's bedroom, where I found her on the floor foaming at the mouth. Lots of empty pill bottles lay scattered around her.

I had attended a huge Catholic cathedral, I had gone to confession, I had genuflected, I had done my rosary—but I only feared God. I was convinced he didn't care about me.

Neither I nor my mother knew that the social worker was coming to place me in your boys home. But I was desperate to get away from my stepfather's abuse, the poverty, and my mother's suicide attempts. So I went along and ended up in your home.

Your house parents were so loving and kind. They taught us Bible studies and took us to church. One day they took us to a little church that was holding a tent revival. I was so bitter inside and so despondent. It was at that little church, under the tent, that the Holy Spirit began tugging at my heart. One night, I couldn't resist any longer. All the years of pain, confusion, and hopelessness came to the surface. I was choking.

Then I heard the preacher say, "Jesus loves you." I got on my knees and prayed, "God, I'm not really sure that you're real, or that you're listening to me. But if you are real, please forgive me, and please help me. I need somebody to love me, because I feel so bitter, rejected, and full of turmoil."

All at once, I felt like somebody was pouring warm molasses on my head and it was flowing down over my body. The bitterness all melted away, God had my heart completely from that day on.

Brother David, that was thirty-five years ago. Now God has called me to preach, and he's moving me into full-time ministry. I found you while surfing the Internet. This thank-you has been brewing in me for thirty-five years. I just want to say thank you for caring, I know what the love of God is.[3]

What if David had not started that boys' home? This young Jewish boy may never have known God's love. Nothing we do for Christ is in vain. This boys' home was not a failure. Though the cost was great, it was worth it because one boy discovered the meaning of God's love.

THREE COMMON *MISUNDERSTANDINGS* ABOUT LOVE

1. Love develops automatically in an unpremeditated way.

An abundance of Bible verses instruct us to love people. Scripture never presumes that we know how to love; rather, over and over again it instructs us to love and explains why we are to love. John was concerned that Christians love one another and that we love those who do not know Christ. Among his many verses on love, he writes,

> "This is how we know who the children of God are and who the children of the devil are; Anyone who does not do what is right is not a child of God; nor is anyone who does not love his brother" (1 John 3:10).

> "We should love one another" (3:11).

> "Anyone who does not love remains in death" (3:14).

"Let us not love with words or tongue but with actions and in truth" (3:18).

"This is his command: to believe in the name of his Son, Jesus Christ, and to love one another as he commanded us" (3:23).

"Dear friends, let us love one another, for love comes from God" (4:7).

"No one has ever seen God; but if we love one another, God lives in us and his love is made complete in us" (4:12).

"Whoever lives in love lives in God" (4:16).

"We love because he first loved us" (4:19).

"I ask that we love one another" (2 John 5).

Joseph Stowell, president of Moody Bible Institute, wrote about an experience he had with news anchor Dan Rather.

Dan Rather was on our campus a couple of years ago to be interviewed on our national radio broadcast *Open Line*. Dan Rather has not been one of my favorite people. I looked at him as part of the left-wing media establishment with its secular, pluralistic, relativistic, anti-God philosophy. He seemed a little cold to me and a touch arrogant, and he was never one of my favorite anchormen. And there he was on our campus.

Well, during a break he and I spent a bit of time together, and I was shocked because he was the warmest individual. He seemed interested in everything I was saying, and he seemed to care about me.

He said, "I grew up in a Baptist home. In my grandma's house the only things she had to read were the Bible and the Sears Roebuck catalog," He continued, "My grandmother read me the Bible every day."

He went back to the interview, and at the close as the tapes were rolling, ready to go nationwide, one of the interviewers said to him, "Mr. Rather, excuse me, I don't want to hurry anything. But if you were to die today and stand before God at the edge of heaven, and God were to say to you, 'Why should I let you into heaven?' What would you say?"

He paused and said, "Well, I have to say it wouldn't be for anything I have done. It would have to be totally by the grace of God."

All of that to say this: I have no idea what his spiritual condition is. This is not a statement about his spiritual condition; it is a statement about a shame I bear in my heart. The shame is it didn't cross my mind once to pray for Dan Rather that God would compassionately reach out and embrace his soul, cancel hell and guarantee heaven, and fill him with abundant living. I hate to tell you that it just never crossed my mind. I was too mad about all this stuff to think about his need for a Savior. I refused to be a middleman in a compassion transaction between God and one who possibly needed him.[4]

In a world full of anger, hate, envy, jealousy, and revenge, we are often influenced to do the same. We must decide every day, however, to be people who are known for how we love.

It is also important to understand that we are people in process. As we grow in our relationship with Christ, we become more like him, more loving. We all have a long way to go, but as disciples, we must continue to grow, develop, and produce more of his fruit.

How can you demonstrate God's love in a situation in which doing so is difficult, nearly impossible? Your action could be the catalyst that causes other people to understand that God wants to help them, or it could persuade them that Christ rules your life.

2. Many people believe that just because they understand the definition of love, they will naturally love.

Understanding a concept and acting on that concept are two different things. We may hear sermons on the four Greek words for love—*erös* (sexual/sensual love), *storgë* (family or natural love), *philë* (friendship love) and *agapë* (God's love). Love, however, is something we *do*. Therefore, we must discipline ourselves to continually practice love.

In his book *The Four Loves*, C. S. Lewis explains the different Greek words that are used for the English word *love*. The Bible often uses the word *agape* when it speaks about God's love for us and the kind of love God wants us to have for others. *Agape* is "that highest and noblest form of love which sees something infinitely precious in its object."[5] Bishop Stephen Neill has defined love as "a steady direction of the will, toward another's lasting good."[6]

Even when we do not feel like loving, we can choose to do so anyway. It is an act of the will, a decision we make. You will find that when you do acts of love regardless of how you feel, you will often develop the "want to." Your emotions will catch on, and eventually compassion will grow in your heart toward that person or group of people.

In his book *The Myth of the Greener Grass*, J. Allan Peterson wrote:

Newspaper columnist and minister George Crane tells of a wife who came into his office full of hatred toward her husband. "I do not only want to get rid of him; I want to get even. Before I divorce him, I want to hurt him as much as he has me."

Dr. Crane suggested an ingenious plan. "Go home and act as if you really love your husband. Tell him how much he means to you. Praise him for every decent trait. Go out of your way to be as kind, considerate, and generous as possible. Spare no efforts to please him, to enjoy him. Make him believe you love him. After you've convinced him of your undying love and that you cannot live without him, then drop the bomb. Tell him that you're getting a divorce. That will really hurt him."

With revenge in her eyes, she smiled and exclaimed, "Beautiful, beautiful. Will he ever be surprised!"

And she did it with enthusiasm. Acting "as if." For two months she showed love, kindness, listening, giving, reinforcing, sharing.

When she didn't return, Crane called. "Are you ready now to go through with the divorce?"

"Divorce!" she exclaimed. "Never! I discovered I really do love him." Her actions had changed her feelings. Motion resulted in emotion. The ability to love is established not so much by fervent promise as often-repeated deeds.[7]

We are to love when we see no results, even when the object of our love continues on his or her path of rejecting, avoiding, or turning against us. Jesus spent much of his last three years with twelve people. He knew that one would be disloyal to him and betray him for money (see Mark 14:10–44; John 6:70–71), yet he continued to minister to him and love him just as he did the other eleven. The fact that Judas was going to commit this act of treason didn't change Jesus' behavior or his love toward Judas. If this is how God treats people who continue to reject him, we should also love in difficult situations. Have you ever gone through a period of time when you disobeyed God? Maybe you totally ignored him. What did he do? He continued to love you and to seek out ways to show you his mercy. We don't love others in the same way as those without Christ love others. Our love should never give up.

Some say, "Well, I'll forgive him for what he did to me, but I won't forget!" Part of what they say is true. It is hard to forget; nevertheless, we must not keep score. If we do, bitterness will infect our hearts and bring great personal injury. Hebrews 12:15 warns us, "See to it . . . that no bitter root grows up to cause trouble and defile many." Your parents, a sibling, a close friend, or your employer may have rejected you. Very possibly you have had the experience of someone betraying you and bringing harm to your reputation or your person. Forgiving that person sets you free and can cause him or her to take note that there is something unique in you.

Jesus will help you. As you cling to him and decide to treat people like he does, your heart will be transformed and God's love will flow through you.

3. Few understand their potential to harm others with words and actions.

Thus they often fail to recognize the times they are unloving—even mean.

One day I (Wayde) received a telephone call from a person who said she and her family would never come back to our church. She was angry and hurt, and she wanted me to know it. I was taken aback by her forcefulness and by the fact that she wanted me to know why she and her family were leaving. Often when people leave a particular church the pastor never knows why. I inquired as to why they had come to this decision. She said,

"We brought a friend to church this week that we had been speaking to for months about his need for God. Finally, he said he would visit our church and see what it was all about.

"We sat in the front row, right in front of you, and were excited about what our friend would think about the service. Shortly after we sat down, one of the ushers came to our friend and said, 'Sir, please remove your cap.'

"Our friend said, 'I'm sorry, but I can't.' The usher then said more firmly, 'Would you please take your cap off?'

"Our friend looked a little embarrassed and shook his head no.

"The usher then said, 'Take off your cap. You are in church!'

"Our friend got up, looked at us, and said, 'I need to leave.' He left, and we followed him to the foyer where we talked."

Although I completely disagreed with the insensitive way the usher had spoken to this man, I asked, "Why didn't your friend want to remove his cap?"

She replied, "Pastor, our friend has leukemia and because of medical treatment has lost most of his hair. He was embarrassed and felt that he looked better with the cap on."

That afternoon, I visited the man and sincerely apologized to him about the conduct at our church. I explained to him that God is always sensitive to our needs and would never want any of his children to treat others this way. I humbly asked him to give us another try. I then asked the usher to call him and apologize.

Our potential for being insensitive to people is huge. Just try to leave the church parking lot after a service and see how often others will let you out before them. How often have you visited a church and had no one speak to you? Have you met greeters who seemed to be doing a job rather than being truly happy to see you and eager to make you feel welcome?

How about you? Do you have your emotions, words, and actions under control? Although most people think they are in control of their lives, outside forces, such as other people, circumstances, politics, the news, or even the weather control them. Our reactions to outside forces demonstrate whether we really are in control. Internal battles may control us as well. Past hurts, rejection, and disappointments constantly nag at us, and we sometimes let our emotional baggage affect how we talk to ourselves and how we treat others.

And how about the church as a whole? Does the world look at the church and see it as an angry church, a church that is constantly picketing, complaining, or demonstrating without compassion? Joseph Stowell said:

> I have never known a time when Christians have been more mad about more things than we are now. . . . We're angry about values, politics, television, media, education, the violation of the unborn, condoms, and criminals. This anger has given rise to a warrior instinct in the Body of Christ that has left us with a radical profile. We're shouting more, and we're shooting at doctors of abortion clinics. Publicly we are perceived to be long on madness and short on mercy, to be more committed to our consternation than we are to compassion.[8]

All of us have a sinful nature, and this nature has tremendous potential to do or say the wrong thing. Paul said, "I die every day—I mean that" (1 Cor. 15:31), meaning that he not only risked his physical life for the sake of the gospel, but he died daily to his sinful nature. It has been said that more people have been killed with the tongue than in all the wars in human history. Words can be as deadly as actions. Our sinful nature, from which these deadly words spring, can be controlled because we are connected to the Vine; however, we need to continually evaluate our attitudes, behavior, and feelings. The Holy Spirit will let us know when we are being unloving, unkind, and unrighteously angry. When he does, we must obey and do the loving thing.

Your love can make a difference. People can change because of the way you treat them. Your words or actions can persuade a depressed person to have hope. What you do can bring encouragement, enrichment, and energy to someone today. If you can't say it, write it. If you feel that you can't do it today, then schedule a time when you can do it. Seldom repress an impulse to do something kind. Our "Godlike" actions could even save a life.

Gary Smalley and John Trent tell the story of a young school-age child who was waiting for a school bus on a cold January morning. Other children who were waiting with him were laughing and playing while Roger stood alone, quiet, looking at the snow-covered ground. When the bus came, the other kids rushed on ahead of him. Roger sat alone in the seat most kids avoided, right behind the bus driver. On the way to school Roger stood up and his books fell to the ground. To balance himself he leaned on the metal pole by the bus door. When the bus driver pulled over to the side of the road and opened the door, Roger stumbled out and fell into the snow—dead.

The autopsy gave no evidence of an obvious reason for Roger's death. Looking deeper into his life, however, may yield an answer. His mother and father had divorced, and his mother had remarried. Roger's stepfather resented his intrusion into their marriage, and his mother spent very little time with him.

Roger began to withdraw from friends at school and became indifferent toward his schoolwork. Gradually, he built a lonely, quiet world around himself. His teachers and friends became weary of trying to understand him and basically left him alone.

Smalley and Trent conclude, "In only a few months, everything and everyone of value to Roger had either been lost or taken from him. With no place of shelter and no words of encouragement, he felt like a cipher—an empty zero. This sensitive child was unable to stand the pain for long. An infirmity or a wound did not kill Roger. He was killed by a lack of words of love and acceptance."[9]

Every person desperately needs love, acceptance, and forgiveness. All around us are people who are similar to Roger. They are in your workplace, school, neighborhood, and, perhaps, family. Your acts of love, words of encouragement, and demonstration of forgiveness could change their lives—for eternity.

LOVE IS POSSIBLE

As we begin the third millennium after Christ, the world most certainly has the greatest technological and scientific advantages of all time and knowledge far beyond the imaginations of people who lived just a hundred years ago. Nevertheless, our age is possibly the most uncontrolled, undisciplined time since before the flood of Noah's day. The philosophy of many lives is, "If it feels good to me, I'm going to find a way to do it." The world is full of compromise concerning morals, integrity, and truth. The thought is, "If it works, I'll keep doing it." Whether what works is moral, just, or true is not the issue—only whether or not it works!

When I (Wayde) was a boy, I lived across the dirt road from a beautiful farm. Often I walked through the fields among the crops, and at times I helped our neighbor bail hay or clean the barn. As you know, animal barns have a distinct odor. No matter how hard the farmer worked at keeping his barn clean, the smell was always there. And no matter how much I avoided getting dirty in the barn, my clothing always smelled like the barn when I went home. Even when my clothes looked clean, my mother would say, "You've been in the barn." Living in this world is like visiting a barn. No matter how much we try to keep the scent of the world off of us, the world still affects us. Thus we have to discipline ourselves to stay close to the one who continually purifies us. Paul's desire for his Thessalonian friends was; "May the Lord make your love increase and overflow for each other and for everyone else. . . . May he strengthen your hearts so that you will be blameless and holy in the presence of our God and Father when our Lord Jesus comes with all his holy ones" (1 Thess. 3:12–13).

You may think this sounds impossible. But if you remain connected to Christ, his supernatural power will work through you, and the world will see that you demonstrate Christ's uniqueness. You will look different to the world because of the fruit you produce. John reminds us that we are to "love one another" and then instructs us that "love comes from God" (1 John 4:7). God's supernatural love that flows through believers is different from the love the world knows and understands. It is such a powerful force that it can "cover over a multitude of sins" (1 Peter 4:8) and drive fear out of our lives, for "there is no fear in love . . . because fear has to do with punishment" (1 John 4:18). When you understand that you have been truly forgiven and that God is constantly trying to demonstrate his love and acceptance toward you, fear fades away. God's love will enable you to forgive yourself and others and help you to stop trying to please people more than God. Depression will scatter, a negative self-image will improve, and the paralysis of self-condemnation will leave when we understand God's incredible love for us. Because we are his creation, we are to love not only others but also ourselves (see James 2:8).

LOVE FORGIVES

The Bible instructs us to "forgive as the Lord forgave you" (Col. 3:13). Jesus even said, "If you forgive men when they sin against you, your heavenly Father will also forgive you. But if you do not forgive men their sins, your Father will not forgive your sins" (Matt. 6:14–15).

For years I did not understand this truth. I wondered how it could be possible for people to forgive some of the offenses that others committed against them. What about those who had been severely physically wounded by another person or those who had been injured by someone's lies about them? What about people who had been molested, abused (physically or emotionally), or raped? The world can be a toxic, hurtful place to live. One out of every three women and one out of every seven men will be abused during their lifetimes. People can use, abuse, and even hate us, yet we are to forgive them.

Why shouldn't we carry a grudge throughout life and hate the people who harm us? Because hating them just brings greater injury to us. We will be bitter, angry people if we walk around with a chip on our shoulders. Unforgiveness binds us and causes our spirit to be negative and impure. God wants us to be free of that. Agnes Sanford said, "As we practice the work of forgiveness we discover more and more that forgiveness and healing are one."[10] We can learn from painful experiences and thereby protect ourselves from future injury; however, we must let go of anger and unforgiveness so that those who have hurt us cannot continue to do so. When we choose to resent someone, we give that person a precious piece of our life. We can take that piece back only by forgiving. Let's get rid of that bondage! Unforgiveness paralyzes us and will greatly hinder our relationship with God. Thomas Adams said, "He who demands mercy, and shows none, ruins the bridge over which he himself must pass."[11] And Henry Ward Beecher said, "Forgiveness ought to be like a cancelled note—torn in two and burned up, so that it never can be shown against one."[12] Christlike forgiveness is possible for us when we are connected to the one who invented forgiveness.

LOVE COMPELS

Jesus said, "I, when I am lifted up from the earth, will draw all men to myself" (John 12:32). His drawing power is his unconditional and sacrificial love. There is no doubt that he was speaking of his imminent death on the cross, an event that must have astonished his followers. Isn't his "dominion . . . an everlasting dominion that will not pass away, and his kingdom . . . one that will never be destroyed" (Dan. 7:14)? Isaiah said, "Of the increase of his government and peace there will be no end" (Isa. 9:7). David also spoke of an endless kingdom: "I will establish your line forever and make your throne firm through all generations" (Ps. 89:4). The Jews wondered how Jesus could be the Messiah whom they knew would establish an everlasting kingdom yet be "lifted up" on a cross. William Barclay provides an answer: "The lesson of history is that Jesus was right. It was on the magnet of the Cross that he pinned his hopes; and he was right because love will live long after might is dead."[13]

In George Bernard Shaw's play *Saint Joan*, when Joan of Arc discovered that she had been betrayed and sentenced by her town's leaders to being burned at the stake, she said, "I will go out now to the common people, and let the love in their eyes comfort me for the hate in yours. You will all be glad to see me burnt; but if I go through the fire, I shall go through it to their hearts for ever and ever."[14] She was saying that the people who loved her would remember her sacrificial death. How much more do we remember the Son of God. Jesus was lifted up on the cruel cross as a sacrificial offering for our sins. His act of love enabled us to be forgiven and to obtain eternal life. His act of love was forever declared to be sufficient to win salvation for you and me.

People hunger to be loved. Many live in shame and guilt or have endured tremendous rejection. Deep down inside they just want to be cared for and loved. They sometimes try to receive love in inappropriate ways, but when they see God's pure, unhesitant, compassionate, and merciful love for them, they are drawn to it. Thus we must let Christ's love flow through us. People will wonder how we can love so; it is because Jesus loves them through us.

LOVE IS RESILIENT

We must attach no conditions to our love. No matter how people treat us, we must keep on loving, forgiving, and praying for them. One of the first martyrs of the church was Stephen. Perhaps the way Stephen died was a wake-up call to Saul who later became Paul. Saul stood nearby and held the outer garments of those who stoned Stephen to death. When Stephen was being stoned he "fell on his knees and cried out, 'Lord, do not hold this sin against them'" (Acts 7:60). Jesus had set an example for Stephen when on the cross he had prayed for his murderers, "Father, forgive them, for they do not know what they are doing" (Luke 23:34).

We must not hold grudges, refuse to "get over it," or attach conditions before we forgive someone. We may be shocked, dazed, or overwhelmed for a time, but we regain our strength because we are attached to the one who supplies abundant love. People will fail us and we will fail people, but if we decide to keep score, no one will win.

Former PTL president and television personality Jim Bakker, who was sent to prison for fraud, wrote in his book *I Was Wrong*,

> Not long after my release from prison, I joined Franklin Graham and his family at his parents' old log mountain home for dinner. Ruth Graham (Billy's wife) had prepared a full-course dinner. We talked and laughed and enjoyed a casual meal together like family.

During our conversation, Ruth asked me a question that required an address. I reached into my back pocket and pulled out an envelope. My wallet had been taken when I went to prison. I had not owned a wallet for over four-and-a-half years.

As I fumbled through the envelope, Ruth asked tenderly, "Don't you have a wallet, Jim?"

"This is my wallet," I replied.

Ruth left the room, returning with one of Billy's wallets. "Here is a brand-new wallet Billy has never used. I want you to have it," she said.

I still carry that wallet to this day. Over the years I have met thousands of wonderful Christian men and women, but never anyone more humble, gracious, and in a word, "real" than Ruth Graham and her family.[15]

In this world people often "write off" people who have let them down or disappointed them. But God's love bounces back. What will you do with the people who have disappointed you? Will you let feelings of resentment, judgment, or anger be a part of your emotions concerning them? Or will you choose to act like Jesus and forgive?

LOVE UNDERSTANDS

We can choose to see through angry, bitter, hateful people's actions and beyond their words to understand that they are likely wounded and trying to protect themselves. If we could go back to the incident that began their angry actions, we would likely see tremendous pain and hurt. God's love understands why they are choosing to act in destructive ways. They think they are protecting themselves from further pain. Their actions repel others because others do not want to get involved in their lives.

When we choose to love hurting, hateful people in spite of their behavior, anger, or rejection, our love often melts their fear of further pain. The process may take a while, but when we love them with God's love they will see that we are different. They will wonder what makes us respond to them differently and why we don't reject them like everyone else does. Our love for them can truly change their lives and can "cover a multitude of sins."

God is love, and we are destined to act like God. In fact, we "are being transformed into his likeness with ever-increasing glory, which comes from the Lord, who is the Spirit" (2 Cor. 3:18).

Jesus looked at the crowds and felt compassion for them. He looked beyond all the activity, noise, and distractions and saw their tremendous need. They were "harassed and helpless, like sheep without a shepherd" (Matt. 9:36). Jesus loved as no human was able to love, he sacrificed as no one ever could, and he forgives beyond our comprehension. There is no way you can love this way unless the Spirit of God helps you. He and he alone will enable you to grow in Christlike love.

CHAPTER 2

JOY

Rejoicing in Any Situation

Have you ever wondered what would make you truly happy? What if all financial restrictions were removed from your life? What if all the people who hold you back were taken out of the way and suddenly you were able to do something that you deeply desired? If you could do what you wanted to do, have what you wanted to have, and be what you wanted to be, would you feel genuine joy?

Most people think, "If only I could . . ." or "if only someone else would . . . ," then I would be happy. A common myth is that the grass is always greener on the other side of the fence; however, when we get there we find it isn't grass—it's just AstroTurf! Husbands walk away from wives because they think being with someone else will make them "really" happy. Wives leave husbands because they think they will be more secure with someone else. People quit decent jobs, change careers, and move across the country thinking that the new job, new house, or the move will bring them the satisfaction and intense happiness they crave. Most, after they make the change, find that they still have to live with *themselves*, and they aren't very happy! Even the United States Declaration of Independence proclaims that we have the right to "the pursuit of happiness." Yet nowhere in the Bible will you find God advising us to pursue happiness. The "happiness" that most seek is disguised as something that will last when in reality it is passing, elusive, or brief.

Is money the key to happiness? Consider what it did for Buddy Post of Oil City, Pennsylvania. In 1988 he won a jackpot of $16.2 million in the Pennsylvania Lottery. That was the beginning of his misery. His landlady claimed that she shared the winning ticket with Post and successfully sued him for one-third of the money. Then he started an assortment of business ventures with his siblings, all of which failed. In 1991 Post was sentenced to six months to two years in prison for assault. Post claimed that he had simply fired a gun into his garage ceiling to scare off his step-daughter's boyfriend, who was arguing with him over business and ownership of Post's pickup. In 1993 Post's brother was convicted of plotting to kill Buddy and his wife to gain access to the lottery money. In 1994 Post filed for bankruptcy. Then Post's wife left him, and the court ordered that Post pay $40,000 a year in support payments.

Post finally had enough. To pay off a mountain of legal fees, he tried in September 1996 to sell off the rights to the seventeen future payments from his jackpot, valued at some $5 million, but the Pennsylvania Lottery tried to block the sale.

"Money didn't change me," says Post. "It changed people around me that I knew, that I thought cared a little bit about me. But they only cared about the money."[1]

God wants us to be full of joy. Joy is part of the fruit of the Spirit package and will be a natural part of our lives when we are connected to the Vine. Like the other fruit of the Spirit, joy is not something we produce on our own. Rather, it is a supernatural result of belonging to the one who is pure joy.

Am I saying that you will be happy all the time, full of laughter, perpetually grinning, and exuberantly excited? No. The joy that the Bible speaks of is much more profound than that. The early church understood that joy would be a reality in their lives no matter what happened to them. When the leaders of the church were beaten, they rejoiced because "they had been counted worthy of suffering disgrace for the Name" (Acts 5:41). James encouraged those who were suffering to endure persecution by writing, "Consider it pure joy . . . whenever you face trials of many kinds, because you know that the testing of your faith develops perseverance" (James 1:2–3). And the writer to the Hebrews inspired the suffering by saying, "Let us fix our eyes on Jesus, the author and perfecter of our faith, who for the joy set before him endured the cross" (Heb. 12:2). Of these early believers Bishop Stephen Neill observed, "It was because they were a joyful people that the early Christians were able to conquer the world."[2]

Joy is much more significant than a happy countenance. True joy, which comes only from the Holy Spirit, is possible even when life is rough, when we are going through great disappointment, loss, or grief. Because of illness, Amy Carmichael was confined to her bed for the last two decades of her life. During this time she wrote numerous books that have helped countless people. She said, "Where the things of God are concerned, acceptance always means the happy choice of mind and heart that He appoints, because (for the present) it is His good and acceptable and perfect will."[3] Amy's situation in life did not take away her sense of joy. She possessed it in spite of her circumstances.

The word Paul uses for joy is *chara*, which most often in the New Testament has a spiritual source, such as "the joy given by the Holy Spirit" (1 Thess. 1:6). The Old Testament often uses phrases like "the joy of the LORD" (Neh. 8:10). And Jesus said he desires that our joy be complete (John 15:11). Pastor and author Jack Hayford describes the concept this way:

> Joy, then, is that ever-deepening awareness that our lives are hidden in Christ and that we can be led by the Spirit through anything. Afflictions, trials, pressures or frustrations may come, but they cannot destroy us; so we experience joy. We may genuinely hurt (2 Cor. 1:8); we may weep (John 11:33–35); we may be tempted (Heb. 2:18); we may not understand what God is allowing to come our way (James 1:2–5); but none of this causes us to lose God's focus in our difficulties or hampers our ministry to the needs of others. "We know that in all things God works for the good of those who love him, who have been called according to his purpose" (Rom. 8:28). This is biblical joy.[4]

COMMON JOY

Some time ago while on vacation in California, my family and I (Wayde) visited the television studios that produce such programs as *The Price Is Right* game show. As we waited to be a part of the audience of one of the other live programs, I watched those who had been selected for *The Price is Right*. Dozens of people sat waiting in anticipation to enter the room where there was a possibility that they would hear their name called along with the words "Come on down!" Several were so happy and excited that they were jumping and laughing in the parking lot, fully expecting that they could win thousands of dollars in cash and prizes that day. I overheard one person telling her friend how she would use the prizes. As the pregame fervor built, many became silly. These people were full of joy.

Both Christians and non-Christians may experience joy in a number of common ways.

Times of Celebration

People are generally happy during the wedding of someone they love, the birth of a baby, a graduation, a job promotion, or an award for a job well done. For most everyone these times are full of rejoicing and celebration.

Times of Achievement

Those who have been able to lose weight, quit a bad habit, walk away from a destructive situation, graduate from college, or finish a difficult job experience a sense of achievement. Goal-orientated people feel a sense of joy and satisfaction when they are able to reach their objective. People who are successful in their chosen career or in raising a family also feel the joy of achievement.

Relationships

Joy may come from having a deep friendship with someone else, such as a spouse, a child, a long-time school friend, or a coworker. Paul Thigpen shared the joy of one such relationship in a *Discipleship Journal* article:

> I remember coming home one afternoon to discover that the kitchen I had worked so hard to clean only a few hours before was now a terrible wreck. My young daughter had obviously been busy "cooking," and the ingredients were scattered, along with dirty bowls and utensils, across the counters and floor. I was not happy with the situation.

Then, as I looked a little more closely at the mess, I spied a tiny note on the table, clumsily written and smeared with chocolatey fingerprints. The message was short—"I'm makin sumthin 4 you, Dad"—and it was signed, "Your Angel."[5]

In the middle of the mess, Paul's irritation and frown turned into joy and a smile. Life's relationships may produce tremendous happiness for Christians and non-Christians alike.

Most relationships involve both give-and-take of emotional energy. We give our expertise, friendship, and care to another person, and they do the same for us when we are in need.

Unexpected Joy

When out of the blue something wonderful happens, we call it a "lucky break" or a "watershed." It could be an unexpected inheritance, a rebate on taxes, or a great deal on something you purchased. The other day I watched a program on which antiques were appraised. A person who had purchased a painting because of the beautiful frame asked the antique expert to appraise the value of the frame. When the trained specialist looked at the picture, he explained to the owner that the painting was several hundred years old and was worth thousands of dollars. Although the frame was valuable, the portrait was worth much more. The owner was obviously pleased, especially since she had paid only a few dollars for the picture at a garage sale. This is an example of unexpected joy that I'm sure most of us would enjoy!

Life Joy

People often experience joy with life itself. Some have mistakenly said that everyone outside of Christianity is unhappy. Actually, a lot of people who are not Christians are basically happy.

In fact, on the surface some non-Christians appear to be more joyful than many Christians. While most everyone can experience a general satisfaction in living, without the unique "joy of the Lord" people are often inwardly miserable. C. S. Lewis wrote in *Mere Christianity*, "God cannot give us a happiness and peace apart from Himself, because it is not there. There is no such thing."[6]

In Frank Minirth and Paul Meier's excellent book *Happiness Is a Choice*, psychologist Paul Meier writes,

> Dr. Minirth and I are convinced that many people do choose happiness but still do not obtain it. The reason for this is that even though they choose to be happy, they seek for inner peace and joy in the wrong places. They seek for happiness in materialism and do not find it. They seek for joy in sexual prowess but end up with fleeting pleasures and bitter long-term disappointments. They seek inner fulfillment by obtaining positions of power in corporations, in government, or even in their own families (by exercising excessive control), but they remain unfulfilled. I have had millionaire businessmen come to my office and tell me they have big houses, yachts, condominiums in Colorado, nice children, a beautiful mistress, an unsuspecting wife, secure corporate positions—and suicidal tendencies. They have everything this world has to offer except one thing—inner peace and joy. They come to my office as a last resort, begging me to help them conquer the urge to kill themselves.[7]

These people obviously aren't happy. The deep, abiding joy that comes only from God isn't present in their lives because they are searching for happiness in things and people other than God. C. S. Lewis said, "Joy is the serious business of heaven."[8]

UNIQUE JOY
FOR THE CHRISTIAN

Theologian William Barclay writes concerning the special joy that Christians sense, "It is not the joy that comes from earthly things, still less from triumphing over someone else in competition. It is a joy whose foundation is God."[9] This joy comes from a relationship with Jesus, the one who is able to give us an eternal perspective no matter what our circumstances. C. S. Lewis said, "Joy is never in our power, and pleasure is. I doubt whether anyone who has tasted joy would ever, if both were in his power, exchange it for all the pleasure in the world."[10]

Rejoice Because You Are Sure of Your Salvation

Knowing that Jesus conquered death for us and purchased our salvation through his precious blood brings a deep sense of joy. Paul said, "[God] has rescued us from the dominion of darkness and brought us into the kingdom of the Son he loves" (Col. 1:13). Before we became believers in Jesus Christ we belonged to Satan's kingdom, but the moment we made Jesus our Lord we were rescued and brought into God's righteous kingdom. Paul also said, "When you were dead in your sins and in the uncircumcision of your sinful nature, God made you alive with Christ. He forgave us all our sins" (Col. 2:13). Christ's salvation not only provides forgiveness of sin but also the power to live righteous lives as children of God.

Jesus used parables to describe to his disciples the value of salvation. On one occasion he said, "Suppose a woman has ten silver coins and loses one. Does she not light a lamp, sweep the house and search carefully until she finds it? And when she finds it, she calls her friends and neighbors together and says, 'Rejoice with me; I have found my lost coin.' In the same way, I tell you, there is rejoicing in the presence of the angels of God over one sinner who repents" (Luke 15:8–10). When Jesus saves us from sin we are like that lost coin that has been found.

Jesus also spoke of the shepherd who had a hundred sheep and lost one of them. "Does he not leave the ninety-nine in the open country and go after the lost sheep until he finds it? And when he finds it, he joyfully puts it on his shoulders and goes home. Then he calls his friends and neighbors together and says, 'Rejoice with me; I have found my lost sheep'" (Luke 15:4–6). Until Jesus finds us we are like that lost sheep. Then when he finds us there is great rejoicing in heaven and in our spirits.

The early believers exhibited the joy of the Lord in all kinds of circumstances. When large numbers of people in Samaria accepted the Word of God and many were delivered from evil spirits and healed of diseases, "there was great joy in the city" (Acts 8:8). When Philip explained the gospel to an Ethiopian eunuch, the man believed in Jesus and "went on his way rejoicing" (Acts 8:39). When a Philippian jailer was about to commit suicide because he thought his prisoners had escaped after an earthquake shook open the jail doors, Paul shouted, "Don't harm yourself! We are all here!" (Acts 16:28). The jailer then asked Paul and his friend Silas (who were two of his prisoners) how to be saved. They explained the gospel to the man and his family and the whole family gave their lives to Christ and were baptized. The Scripture says that "he was filled with joy because he had come to believe in God—he and his whole family" (Acts 16:34).

Only those who have been born again can fully understand this unique kind of joy, because it is heavenly, not earthly. It comes from the one who created you as your heart seeks ways to worship him. Methodist Bishop Ralph Spaulding Cushman articulated the joy of worshiping the Creator in these words:

> Oh the sheer joy of it!
> Living with Thee,

31

God of the universe,
Lord of a tree,
Maker of mountains,
Lover of me!
Oh the sheer joy of it!
Breathing Thy air;
Morning is dawning,
Gone every care,
All the world's singing
"God's everywhere!"
Oh the sheer joy of it!
Walking with Thee,
Out on the hilltop,
Down by the sea,
Life is so wonderful,
Life is so free.
Oh the sheer joy of it!
Working with God,
Running His errands,
Wanting His nod,
Building His heaven
On common sod.
Oh the sheer joy of it!
Ever to be
Living in glory,
Living with Thee,
Lord of tomorrow,
Lover of me![11]

Increase Your Joy by Leading Others to Jesus Christ

Incredible satisfaction and joy come from personally explaining the gospel to someone and seeing that person give his or her life to Christ. The early church became "very glad" when they heard that the Gentiles had been converted (see Acts 15:3). If heaven rejoices over one sinner who repents (Luke 15:7) and if angels become excited because a person decides to follow Christ (v. 10), then we ought to feel tremendous joy when we have the privilege of introducing someone to Jesus.

The great evangelist D. L. Moody said,

> I believe that if an angel were to wing his way from earth up to Heaven, and were to say that there was one poor, ragged boy, without a father or mother, with no one to care for him and teach him the way of life; and if God were to ask who among them was willing to come down to this earth and live here for fifty years and lead that one to Jesus Christ, every angel in Heaven would volunteer to go. Even Gabriel, who stands in the presence of the Almighty, would say, "Let me leave my high and lofty position, and let me have the luxury of leading one soul to Jesus Christ." There is no greater honor than to be the instrument in God's hands of leading one person out of the kingdom of Satan into the glorious light of Heaven.[12]

Realize How Present-Day Battles Can Contribute to Your Eternal Destiny

A unique difference between those who know Christ and those who do not ought to be their ability to see the value of, and even welcome, suffering when it comes. James said, "Consider it pure joy, my brothers, whenever you face trials of many kinds" (James 1:2). Trials, stress, and suffering are not good in themselves, but they can, however, strengthen character. Paul said, "We . . . rejoice in our sufferings, because we know that suffering produces perseverance; perseverance, character; and character, hope" (Rom. 5:3).

Through the trials of life we can choose to mature and grow in our faith. Some make the decision to become angry or bitter when life's difficulties and sorrows come, while others choose to look to God and find a way to grow. Joni Eareckson Tada, a woman who knows something about suffering, since she was paralyzed in a diving accident in her youth, said, "With profound potential for good, suffering can also be a destroyer. Suffering can pull families together, uniting them through hardship, or it can rip them apart in selfishness and bitterness. Suffering can file all the rough edges off your character, or it can further harden you. It all depends. On us. On how we respond."[13] Our suffering can have eternal value and can bring a depth of character that nothing else in life can bring.

The story is told of a man who found the cocoon of an emperor moth and took it home to watch it emerge. One day a small opening appeared, and for several hours the moth struggled but couldn't seem to force its body past a certain point.

Deciding something was wrong, the man took scissors and snipped the remaining bit of cocoon. The moth emerged easily, its body large and swollen, the wings small and shriveled.

The man expected that in a few hours the wings would spread out in their natural beauty, but they did not. Instead of developing into a creature free to fly, the moth spent its life dragging around a swollen body and shriveled wings.

The constricting cocoon and the struggle necessary to pass through the tiny opening are God's way of forcing fluid from the body into the wings. The "merciful" snip was in reality cruel. Sometimes the struggle is exactly what we need.[14]

Do you see any value in your suffering? Rejoice, because only through suffering can you acquire a depth of maturity that will make you more like Christ.

The words of Malcolm Muggeridge speak volumes of wisdom to those who wonder why suffering needs to be part of maturity.

Contrary to what might be expected, I look back on experiences that at the time seemed especially desolating and painful, with particular satisfaction. Indeed, I can say with complete truthfulness that everything I have learned in my seventy-five years in this world, everything that has truly enhanced and enlightened my existence, has been through affliction and not through happiness, whether pursued or attained. In other words, if it ever were to be possible to eliminate affliction from our earthly existence by means of some drug or other medical mumbo jumbo. . . . the result would not be to make life delectable, but to make it too banal or trivial to be endurable. This of course is what the cross signifies, and it is the cross more than anything else, that has called me inexorably to Christ.[15]

People sometimes get the idea that if they will just give their lives to Christ, they will no longer experience problems and difficulties. But suffering is part of life, and the Bible gives us numerous examples of godly people who endured tremendous pain and suffering.

John Ortberg writes in his book *The Life You've Always Wanted*,

We all live with the illusion that joy will come someday when conditions change. We go to school and think we will be happy when we graduate. We are single and are convinced we will be happy when we get married. We get married and decide we will be happy someday when we have children. We have children and decide we will be happy when they grow up and leave the nest—then they do, and we think we were happier when they were still at home.

"This is God's day," the psalmist says. It is the day God made, a day that Christ's death has redeemed. If we are going to know joy, it must be this day—today.

But this raises the question. How can I embrace joy amid all the pain and suffering in the world? Is it right to be joyful in a world of hunger and violence and injustice?

It is precisely here that we make one of the most surprising discoveries: Often it is the people closest to suffering who have the most powerful joy. Friends of Mother Teresa say that instead of being overwhelmed by the suffering around her, she fairly glows with joy as she goes about her ministry of mercy. One of the English officers imprisoned at Flossenburg with Dietrich Bonhoeffer said of him, "Bonhoeffer always seemed to me to spread an atmosphere of happiness and joy over the least incident and profound gratitude for the mere fact that he was alive."

True joy, as it turns out, comes only to those who have devoted their lives to something greater than personal happiness. This is most visible in extraordinary lives, in saints and martyrs. But is no less true for ordinary people like us.

One test of authentic joy is its compatibility with pain. Joy in this world is always joy "in spite of" something. Joy is, as Karl Barth put it, a "defiant nevertheless" set at a full stop against bitterness and resentment.

If we don't rejoice today, we will not rejoice at all. If we wait until conditions are perfect, we will still be waiting when we die. If we are going to rejoice, it must be in this day.[16]

Rejoice When God Is Glorified

Paul said, "Whatever you do, do it all for the glory of God" (1 Cor. 10:31). One of the greatest joys a person can have in life is to know that he or she is bringing glory to God. It could be through the decision to walk away from a sinful temptation or through a commitment to do the right thing even when the personal cost is high. It could come because someone is consciously looking for ways to bring glory to God as he or she walks through the day.

Every Christian should have a driving motivation to bring glory to God in all he or she does.

During the years when Michael Jordan led the Chicago Bulls to several national championships, many things motivated him. One was that fifty-year-old Frank Hamblen, who had come to the Bulls as assistant coach in 1997, had served various teams for twenty-five years but did not own a championship ring.

That year the Bulls were pursuing their fifth championship. Jordan told writer Melissa Isaacson of the *Chicago Tribune*, "[Hamblen's] been around the league for so long, on a lot of teams and made some great contributions . . . and then not to be on a championship team. . . . That will be my gift to Hamblen. That's part of my motivation."

Hamblen said, "Michael came to me early in the season and told me it was a big motivation for him to win so that I can get a ring. When the best basketball player in the world tells you that, well, it certainly made me feel special."

Chicago won it all in 1997, and Frank Hamblen got his championship ring.[17]

The Christian's greatest motivation and desire in life should be to bring glory to God. Every day we can wake up and say to our God, "Today, I want to bring glory to you in everything I say and do." We can do that by purposing to be obedient in all he asks us to do.

Increase Your Joy by Being Filled with the Holy Spirit

The great evangelist D. L. Moody said, "God commands us to be filled with the Spirit, and if we are not filled, it is because we are living beneath our privileges."[18] People who have been filled with the Holy Spirit can have such joy that someone could come to the conclusion that they are intoxicated (see Acts 2:13). The filling of the Spirit provides a cleansing accompanied by boldness and power to be more effective in witnessing. This experience in turn brings a deep sense of happiness to those who have received it. Charles G. Finney said of his experience, "The Holy Spirit descended upon me in a manner that seemed to go through me, body and soul. I could feel the impression like a wave of electricity going through and through me. Indeed, it seemed to come in waves and waves of liquid love . . . like the very breath of God . . . it seemed to fan me like immense wings."[19]

When the believers in the upper room were filled with the Holy Spirit on the Day of Pentecost, those who observed wanted to know if and how they could have the same experience. Peter told them, "The promise is for you and your children and for all who are far off—for all whom the Lord our God will call" (Acts 2:39).

The Holy Spirit is grieved when believers ignore his conviction for sinful thinking, feelings, or behavior and push aside his warning to act or think differently. But when we repent and determine to be obedient to the Lord, we can ask God to fill us with the Holy Spirit. His filling can be repeated whenever we feel spiritually dry or our boldness to witness has turned to fear. He promises to bring "times of refreshing" (see Acts 3:19) to our tired souls.[20]

DO YOU HAVE JOY?

What makes you happy? Is it what you own, where you live, what group you are included in? Or is it being born again and having the gift of eternal life that makes you happy? Are you joyful because God is glorified in the way you live and because Christ has filled you with the Holy Spirit? Malcolm Muggeridge said, "I can say that I never knew what joy was until I gave up pursuing happiness, or cared to live until I chose to die. For these two discoveries I am beholden to Jesus."[21]

G. K. Chesterton wrote in his book *Orthodoxy,*

Joy which was the small publicity of the pagan, is the gigantic secret of the Christian. And as I close this chaotic volume I open again the strange small book from which all Christianity came; and I am again haunted by a kind of confirmation. The tremendous figure, which fills the Gospels, towers in this respect, as in every other, above all the thinkers who ever thought themselves tall. His pathos was natural, almost casual. The Stoics, ancient and modern, were proud of concealing their tears. He never concealed His tears; He showed them plainly on His open face at any daily sight, such as the far sight of His native city. Yet He concealed something. Solemn supermen and imperial diplomatists are proud of restraining their anger. He never restrained His anger. He flung furniture down the front steps of the Temple, and asked men how they expected to escape the damnation of Hell. Yet He restrained something. I say it with reverence; there was in that shattering personality a thread that must be called shyness. There was something that He hid from all men when He went up a mountain to pray. There was something that He covered constantly by abrupt silence or impetuous isolation. There was some one thing that was too great for God to show us when He walked upon our earth; and I have sometimes fancied that it was His mirth.[22]

Chesterton may be right. We simply cannot fully express the insurmountable joy and eternal satisfaction that belongs to us as believers in Jesus Christ. Our greatest earthly pleasure is only a small touch of what we will experience in heaven's eternity. Our unique joy begins with the fact that Christ lives within us, we belong to him, and we are eternally alive in him. This joy the world can never understand.

CHAPTER 3

PEACE

Overcoming Anxiety and Conflict

Moving from volcano and earthquake country to tornado country required my (Wayde) family to adjust our thinking. In Seattle we frequently heard predictions of what would happen if Mount Rainier erupted, and the frightening memory of the eruption of Mount Saint Helens is very much alive throughout the Pacific Northwest. We were used to the idea that a mountain might blow or an earthquake could happen somewhere along one of the faults that ripple through the West Coast. Tornadoes are different. They have similar devastating results, but the threat comes from above the ground rather than below.

In the final scene of *Twister* an F5 tornado over a mile wide chases the two main characters, Bill and Jo, as they run for their lives. They first seek safety in an old barn, but the fierce winds pick up metal objects in the barn and hurl them through the air like knives. Next, they race to an old pump house and fasten themselves with leather straps to some pipes that go thirty feet underground.

When the tornado moves over them, it rips the pump house from its foundation and carries it away in a swirling black mass. Then the twister tries to draw them upward into its core, but as they cling desperately to the pipes, the leather straps keep them anchored to the earth. After the tornado finally passes, the camera looks down on the scene from high in the air. Although there is an enormous path of destruction many miles long and over a mile wide, for some reason an old farmhouse stands alone and undisturbed.

Though the story is fictional, the thought came to me that the scene is much like the experiences we have throughout life. Storms come and go—bad things happen to good people, and wonderful, godly people experience tragedy (just ask Job), but for the believer there is peace. The Bible never promises that we will escape the storms of life; it does, however, promise us peace and protection in the midst of those storms.

Peace is the third portion of the fruit of the Spirit listed in Galatians 5:22–23. Every human heart yearns for it. Jesus promised his disciples, "Peace I leave with you; my peace I give you" (John 14:27). The Greek word for peace *(eirēnē)* in this verse means more than living a life with no conflict or being quiet, still, and at rest. It is used for the calmness that a nation or city enjoys when it has a caring, competent, and secure leader. William Barclay writes that in biblical times "villages had an official who was called the superintendent of the village's *eirēnē*, the keeper of public peace."[1] Having this kind of peace means having tranquillity in your heart that originates from the understanding that your life is truly in the hands of a loving God. It means experiencing quiet in your inner self.

Don't misunderstand. Having peace doesn't mean that you will not have conflict, stress, or difficult times. For some, becoming Christians and living godly lives have brought more difficulty (persecution) than they would have experienced as non-Christians. While in prison Paul wrote, "I have learned to be content whatever the circumstances" (Phil. 4:11). When the fruit of peace is produced within us by the Holy Spirit, we can live life to the fullest in harmony and tranquillity in spite of our circumstances. As we learn to depend on the Holy Spirit and understand that he will be with us in every situation, we will be more at rest and anxiety will be further away.

In the children's book (which is really a book for every age) *The Velveteen Rabbit*, Margery Williams tells the imaginary story of a stuffed rabbit who came to life because its owner loved it. The following is a conversation between the rabbit and the toy riding horse.

"What is REAL?" asked the rabbit one day, when they were lying side by side near the nursery fender, before Nana came to tidy the room. "Does it mean having things that buzz inside you and stick-out handles?"

"Real isn't how you are made," said the Skin Horse. "It's a thing that happens to you. When a child loves you for a long, long time, not just to play with, but REALLY loves you, then you become Real."

"Does it hurt?" asked the Rabbit.

"Sometimes," said the Skin Horse, for he was always truthful. "When you are Real you don't mind being hurt."

"Does it happen all at once, like being wound up," he asked, "or bit by bit?"

"It doesn't happen all at once," said the Skin Horse. "You become. It takes a long time. That's why it doesn't often happen to people who break easily, or have sharp edges, or who have to be carefully kept. Generally, by the time you are Real, most of your hair has been loved off, and your eyes drop out and you get loose in the joints and very shabby. But these things don't matter at all, because once you are Real you can't be ugly, except to people who don't understand."[2]

As we grow in our relationship with Christ and realize that he is always loving us, praying for us, and caring for us, our deep sense of peace will be more consistent in whatever life brings. While in a very difficult place in life, Paul wrote, "The peace of God, which transcends all understanding, will guard your hearts and minds in Christ Jesus" (Phil. 4:7). Thus we can see that our peace comes from the one to whom we are connected. And therefore unbelievers cannot experience or understand the peace believers enjoy.

Peace doesn't come as a result of changing our circumstances. Rather, it is a supernatural power that flows through us and pushes out turmoil, worry, and anxiety. Immediately upon becoming Christians we sense peace in our lives. But because of life's battles, trials, and difficulties, our focus can be thrown off. That is probably why Paul wrote in Colossians 3:15–16 that we are to "let the peace of Christ rule in [our] hearts" and "let the word of Christ dwell in [us] richly." We must not allow life's circumstances to take away our peace. Rather, we must determine to cling to the promises of God's Word so that our hearts and minds are guarded from worry. With time, maturity, and a growing trust in God, we can learn to be "content whatever the circumstances."

In all of Paul's thirteen letters he writes, "Grace and peace to you." Not once does he say, "Peace and grace to you." It is as if he is saying that people can never begin to experience true peace until they have experienced God's grace through salvation. Paul desires that his brothers and sisters grow in God's grace, because he is certain that the more people understand God's rich grace, mercy, and forgiveness, the more they will live a life that will be unruffled by life's circumstances. God's peace transcends the understanding of the world, other religions, and psychological theories; only those in whom the Holy Spirit dwells can truly understand it.

TRUE PEACE BEGINS WHEN A PERSON MEETS THE "PRINCE OF PEACE" (ISA. 9:6)

Popular radio commentator Paul Harvey tells the fascinating story of a boy named John who lived in the eighteenth century.

When John was eleven, his father—a master of a ship in the Mediterranean trade—took the boy on board.

The early training provided excellent groundwork for John's next major seafaring experience, impressment into the British Navy.

Yet what John had gained from his father's knowledge of sailing, he had lost in discipline. John was soon arrested for desertion, publicly flogged and demoted to common sailor.

At twenty-one, John hopped on an outbound ship from the African coast called the *Greyhound*, on which he presently returned to the depravity of his teens.

Associating with the lowest of crew members, John ridiculed the upright seamen in his company, ridiculed the ship's captain—even ridiculed a book he had found on board. A book entitled *The Imitation of Christ*. Clearly, he remembered joking about that book one bright afternoon.

That night the *Greyhound* sailed into a violent storm. John awakened to discover his cabin filled with seawater. The ship's side had caved in and the *Greyhound* was going down. The *Greyhound* had sailed into high seas; her side collapsed in the turbulence.

Ordinarily such damage would send a ship to the bottom within a few minutes. In this case, the Greyhound's buoyant cargo bought a few hours of precious time.

After nine hours at the pumps, John overheard a desperate remark from one of the crew. They were all goners, he said.

And almost in answer, John—unwittingly and for the first

time in his life—prayed. "If this will not do, the Lord have mercy on us!"

The record shows that the *Greyhound* did not go down.

Although one might have expected John's prayer of emergency to be quickly forgotten, it was remembered unto his death. Each year he observed the anniversary of that most significant incident with prayer and fasting. In a very real sense, he observed it throughout each remaining day of his life.

For John retired from the sea to become a minister. Also a writer of verse.[3]

John's last name was Newton. He is the man who wrote the words to the ever-popular song "Amazing Grace."

> *Amazing grace! How sweet the sound,*
> *That saved a wretch like me!*
> *I once was lost, but now am found,*
> *Was blind, but now I see.*

As believers in Jesus Christ we have a peace that those without Christ can never know. No other religious leader—not the Dalai Lama, a Mormon bishop, a New Age guru, or Mohammed himself—can give the kind of peace Jesus gives. He said, "In me you may have peace" (John 16:33).

PEACE CAN REPLACE WORRY AND ANXIETY IN YOUR LIFE

Garrison Keillor, author of *Lake Wobegon Days*, writes that his greatest fear as a child was getting his tongue stuck on a frozen pump handle. The older boys told him that if he touched his tongue to a pump handle, the only way to get him loose would be to rip his tongue out of his mouth or else put a tent over him until spring.[4] Though this may sound humorous, I can identify with this kind of worry, because I grew up in Minnesota.

One of the most common uncomfortable emotions with which we struggle is anxiety. Anxiety and worry are twins. Some people worry more than others, but we all have had times when we worried too much. We may wake up in the middle of the night with thoughts of what might happen tomorrow. Some may panic over what might go wrong at an important meeting, and their fear may cause them to be forgetful, feel ill, or even avoid the meeting entirely. The word *worry* comes from the German word *wergen*, which means, "to choke." Have you ever heard someone say, "He choked"? Because of his lack of peace, he really might have. "Anxiety disorders (frequent and intense anxiety) affect 20 to 30 million Americans. It is the number-one mental health problem for women and the number-two for men."[5]

Jesus said, "Do not worry about your life . . . Who of you by worrying can add a single hour to his life? . . . Therefore do not worry about tomorrow, for tomorrow will worry about itself" (Matt. 6:25, 27, 34).

Worry and peace can't live together; they are opposites. Corrie ten Boom said, "Worry is a cycle of inefficient thoughts whirling around a center of fear. . . . Worry doesn't empty tomorrow of its sorrow; it empties today of its strength."[6] Chuck Swindoll said, "We all know what worry is. It's when we pay the interest on trouble before the bill comes due. As someone once put it, worry is like a thin stream of fear trickling through the mind. If encouraged, it cuts a channel into which all other thoughts are drained.'"[7] Worry is a waste of time and will take your joy, peace, contentment, confidence, and energy. God's peace, on the other hand, will enhance all you do.

I love the story of Jesus and his disciples crossing the lake in a fishing boat. A violent windstorm came up (see Luke 8:23). The disciples became fearful and "woke him, saying, 'Master, Master, we're going to drown!'" The amazing thing to me is that they needed to wake him up. After all, most of the disciples were experienced fishermen and had been in rough waters before. Nevertheless, this storm greatly rattled them. Jesus, however, was sleeping soundly. Why? Because Jesus understood something his disciples didn't understand at that time. He could trust his Father in every situation. The storm wasn't going to kill them. In fact, Jesus spoke to the storm and it let up.

Years later Peter, who had been in the boat with Jesus, was imprisoned and was to appear before King Herod. The night before the trial "Peter was sleeping" (Acts 12:6). An "angel of the Lord appeared and a light shone in the cell. He struck Peter on the side and woke him up" (v. 7). The angel then led Peter past two sets of guards, through an iron gate (that opened by itself), and into the streets of the city. This story of God's deliverance is powerful. Another amazing fact, however, is that the night before Peter was to receive a death sentence, he was asleep. Peter had learned from his Master that when the storms of life came, he could be at peace. Worry would not help the situation at all.

What is the key to being at peace when life gets complicated? Trust. If we want to experience God's peace in all of life's challenges, we must learn to trust God. The writer of Proverbs instructs us to "trust in the LORD with all your heart and lean not on your own understanding; in all your ways acknowledge him, and he will make your paths straight" (3:5–6). *Trust, lean not,* and *acknowledge* are directive words. They are telling us to "just do it!" God's promise is that he "will make your paths straight." If we pray, obey God's Word, work hard at what we do, and trust God, we won't waste time worrying. Instead, we will rest in the fact that God dearly loves us and will take care of us.

PEACE CAN REPLACE HOSTILITY AND ANGER IN OUR LIFE

Henry Drummond writes in The Greatest Thing in the World,

> No form of vice, not worldliness, not greed of gold, not drunkenness itself, does more to unchristianize society than evil temper. For embittering life, for breaking up communities, for destroying the most sacred relationships, for devastating homes, for withering up men and women, for taking the bloom of childhood, in short, for sheer gratuitous misery-producing power this influence stands alone.[8]

All of us have had to deal with personal anger. Some of us have grown up in homes where out-of-control anger resulted in abuse. People sometimes excuse their anger by claiming that they are Irish or Italian or hot-blooded or redheaded. But anger has nothing to do with one's ethnicity, blood temperature, or hair color—everyone gets angry. And unless it is controlled by the peace of God, anger can devour your happiness, steal your joy, attack your health, destroy your relationships, and injure your faith. Anger in itself is not wrong; it's the way we choose to display our anger that is often wrong. Paul cautioned, "In your anger do not sin" (Eph. 4:26).

There is no doubt that unrighteous, out-of-control anger will destroy your peace. Derrald Vaughn, Ph.D., psychologist and professor at Bethany College in Scotts Valley, California, suggests ten ways to control anger.[9]

1. Realize anger is one of the emotions God gave you and is not a sin in itself. If you have something to be upset about, you can communicate it, and probably should, before the problem gets worse.

49

2. Acknowledge that being hot-blooded, a redhead, or someone who needs to vent feelings are not plausible excuses for outbursts.

3. Realize actions are controlled by the will, so you can decide to control anger's behavior. You can stop and pray for help. Sometimes anger should be vented to God alone. Or you can write a letter and destroy it. You can take anger out by doing housework or washing the car.

4. Decide what is important to be angry about. Don't bother with spilled milk, scratched furniture, dented cars, or money. With children, get upset with rebellion, disobedience, lying, breaking the Ten Commandments, or other things that will hurt the child or someone else. To find appropriate places for anger, study the Bible and pray for wisdom.

5. Use anger constructively, but accept what cannot be changed. We must not take matters into our own hands, however. Bombing an abortion clinic is inappropriate use of anger because it breaks the same commandment abortionists are breaking; it is not righteous indignation. Anger at Satan's work should take us to our knees to intercede for family, friends, neighbors, and nations; cause us to volunteer to teach Sunday school, visit the sick, love the broken, and feed the hungry; and motivate us to vote and speak out on moral matters.

6. Humble yourself and listen to other people. Much anger is caused by pride—you think you are always right and know better than anyone else does.

7. Ask forgiveness from those offended by your angry outbursts. Sometimes we use anger inappropriately because we are rewarded for it temporarily. In the long run, however, it doesn't solve problems.

8. Forgive those who cause anger.

9. Avoid substances that promote anger and investigate other causes of your anger. For example, alcohol affects inhibitory pathways in the brain, sometimes causing angry outbursts, violence, and even murder. Recent research has found drinking is the number one predictor of physical and sexual abuse. Grief may also be a factor, because anger is a stage in the grieving process for any loss.

10. Cultivate the fruit of the Spirit. When you are filled with love, joy, peace, patience, kindness, goodness, faithfulness, gentleness, and self-control, you will have little room for inappropriate use of anger.

When we decide that we are going to let peace rule our lives and not inappropriately react to life's challenges, the fruit of the Spirit will be enhanced.

PEACE WILL ENABLE YOU TO RESOLVE STRESS

Director of the future Health Study Center in Menomonie, Wisconsin, Richard Swenson, M.D., reports:

- In the United States, 30 million men describe themselves as being stressed out.
- The average desk worker has thirty-six hours of work on his/ her desk and spends three hours a week sorting the piles.
- The average middle manager is interrupted seventy-three times a day.
- Fifty percent of managers say the uncontrolled flood of information constitutes a major stressor in the workplace every day; 95 percent say it won't improve.
- "Moonlighting" and overtime in America are at record levels.

- Men average forty-seven hours a week at work. Two-thirds of married women working outside the home work sixty-five to eighty-five hours a week including their domestic hours at home.
- American workers put in more hours on the job than any other industrialized country surveyed, averaging 280 more hours a year than the Germans.
- We spend eight months of our lives opening junk mail.
- We spend one year searching for misplaced objects.
- We spend two years of our lives trying to call people who aren't in or whose lines are busy.
- Eighteen million Americans take the antidepressant Prozac.[10]

In my work with ministers I have a growing awareness that if they do not somehow bring balance into their lives they may experience marital difficulty, more rebellion by their children, and burnout. One executive who works with missionary candidates said, "We are now getting missionary candidates who are beginning their careers burned-out."

In the 1960s those who predicted the future advantages of technology and innovation felt the biggest challenge to the future would be boredom. They believed that time-saving technologies would increase productivity, and they informed a Senate subcommittee that in 1985 people would work approximately twenty-two hours a week, twenty-seven weeks a year, and would retire at age thirty-eight.[11] We now look at those numbers and laugh!

I have a concern for the average growing family in the church. The average husband and wife unit is currently working ninety to one hundred hours a week. Families are taking such heavy hits because of excessive business commitments that they are not bored but exhausted.

How can we get control of the stress of our lives and find

balance? When Jesus was born the angels announced to the shepherds; "Glory to God in the highest, and *on earth peace* to men on whom his favor rests" (Luke 2:14, emphasis added). In the midst of your frantic lifestyle Jesus can speak to you about balance, rest, and peace. Paul said, "We are hard pressed on every side, but not crushed; perplexed, but not in despair; persecuted, but not abandoned; struck down, but not destroyed" (2 Cor. 4:8–9). How did he handle such stress? His secret is found in verse 7: "We have this treasure in jars of clay to show that this all-surpassing power is from God and not from us." The treasure he spoke of is "the light of the knowledge of the glory of God" (v. 6). We are the "jars of clay." The amazing treasure in our person is our relationship with Jesus and the knowledge we have of God's glory.

Philip Hughes tells in his commentary on 2 Corinthians about what he believes Paul was speaking of when he used the words "jars of clay" and "treasure":

> It was not unusual for the most precious treasures to be concealed in mean and valueless containers. In Roman triumphal processions, also, it was customary for gold and silver to be carried in earthen vessels. Thus Plutarch describes how, at the celebration of the Macedonian victory of Aemilius Paulus in 167 B.C., three thousand men followed the wagons carrying silver coins in seven hundred and fifty earthen vessels, each containing three talents and borne by four men. . . . It was very possibly [Paul's] intention here to suggest a picture of the victorious Christ entrusting his riches to the poor earthen vessels of his human followers.[12]

You have a treasure. In spite of the tremendous stress in your life, you can find balance. But you must take time to let Jesus help you with the load you are carrying. He will speak to you when you pray. He will communicate truth to you when you read his Word. And he will instruct you about how to prioritize your life.

PEACE IN THE MIDST OF CRISES

Hurricanes are fierce, powerful, catastrophic storms that can move at speeds in excess of a hundred miles per hour. The waves and rain that accompany hurricanes have deluged many coastal communities and destroyed thousands of homes and businesses over the years. In the eye of a hurricane, however, it is calm—even tranquil.

Psalm 46 says,

> God is our refuge and strength,
>   an ever-present help in trouble.
> Therefore we will not fear, though the earth give way
>   and the mountains fall into the heart of the sea,
>   though its waters roar and foam
>   and the mountains quake with their surging. . . .
> "Be still, and know that I am God;
>   I will be exalted among the nations,
>   I will be exalted in the earth."
>
> The Lord Almighty is with us.
> (vv. 1–3,10–11)

Everyone will have times of crisis. Christian counselor and author H. Norman Wright says in his book *Crisis Counseling* that "the journey through life is a series of crises—some are predictable and expected and some are total surprises. Some crisis is developmental and some are situational. . . . Being alive means that

PEACE

we constantly have to resolve problems. Every new situation we encounter provides the opportunity to develop new ways of using our resources to gain control."[13]

One tremendous benefit of crisis situations in life is that they can force us into a place of brokenness concerning our own strength and lead us to dependence on the power of God. We often need to utterly rely on him to sustain us and give us wisdom to go through our times of need.

Chuck Swindoll said,

Crisis crushes. And in crushing, it often refines and purifies. You may be discouraged today because the crushing has not yet led to surrender. I've stood beside too many of the dying, ministered to too many of the broken and bruised to believe that crushing is an end in itself. Unfortunately, however, it usually takes the brutal blows of affliction to soften and penetrate hard hearts. Even though such blows seem unfair.

Alexander Solzhenitsyn reflected on his unjust time in prison and said, "It was only when I lay there on rotting prison straw that I sensed within myself the first stirring of good. Gradually, it was disclosed to me that the line separating good and evil passes, not through states, nor between classes, nor between political parties either, but right through all human hearts. So, bless you, prison, for having been in my life."[14]

Whenever crisis comes we can know that Jesus Christ is right there with us, for he said, "I am with you always" (Matt. 28:20). The writer of Hebrews reminds us that "God has said, 'Never will I leave you; never will I forsake you'" (13:5). We have a relationship with the living Jesus Christ and can go to him, talk to him, and depend on him to give us a unique peace even in times of crisis.

For years Ira Sankey had the opportunity to be the worship

55

leader for evangelist D. L. Moody. During that time Sankey had the opportunity to become friends with Horatio Gates Spafford who wrote the familiar hymn "It Is Well with My Soul." Sankey reveals the amazing background behind the meaning of its words.

When Mr. Moody and I were holding meetings in Edinburgh, in 1874, we heard the sad news of the loss of the French steamer *Ville de Havre* on her return from America to France with a large number of members of the Ecumenical Council, whose meetings had been held in Philadelphia. On board the steamer was a Mrs. Spafford, with her four children. In mid-ocean a collision took place with a large sailing vessel, causing the steamer to sink in half an hour. Nearly all on board were lost. Mrs. Spafford got her children out of their berths and up on the deck. On being told that the vessel would soon sink, she knelt down with her children in prayer, asking God that they might be saved if possible; or be made willing to die, if that was his will. In a few minutes the vessel sank to the bottom of the sea, and the children were lost. One of the sailors of the vessel, named Lockurn—whom I afterward met in Scotland—while rowing over the spot where the vessel disappeared, discovered Mrs. Spafford floating in the water. Ten days later she was landed at Cardiff, Wales. From there she cabled to her husband, a lawyer in Chicago, the message, "Saved alone." Mr. Spafford, who was a Christian, had the message framed and hung up in his office. He started immediately for England to bring his wife to Chicago. Mr. Moody left his meetings in Edinburgh and went to Liverpool to comfort the bereaved parents and was greatly pleased to find that they were able to say: "It is well; the will of God be done."

In 1876, when we returned to Chicago to work, I was entertained at the home of Mr. and Mrs. Spafford for a number of weeks. During that time Mr. Spafford wrote the hymn "It

Is Well with My Soul" in commemoration of the death of his children. P. P. Bliss composed the music and sang it for the first time at a meeting in Farwell Hall. The comforting fact in connection with this incident was that in one of our small meetings in North Chicago, a short time prior to their sailing for Europe, the children had been converted.[15]

Through the pages of time, many have gone through this kind of crisis. In the middle of the most difficult time in his life Horatio Spafford found peace, comfort, and the words to express the trust and peace in his heart.

> *When peace like a river attendeth my way,*
> *When sorrows like sea-billows roll;*
> *Whatever my lot, Thou has taught me to say,*
> *It is well, it is well with my soul.*

GOD'S PEACE ENCOURAGES US TO BE PEACEMAKERS

In his Bible study guide on peace, Jack Kuhatschek tells about a friend's experience.

One day a man dumped a large load of garbage into the creek behind the house of a friend of mine. As my friend was cleaning up the soggy mess, he noticed an envelope with the man's name and address on it. He promptly loaded up the garbage and drove to the man's house. Just as the man was coming out of his front door, my friend dumped the entire pile of garbage into his front yard. The man stood there, dumbfounded as my friend drove away laughing.[16]

We may all have had a similar experience in which we desperately wanted to repay someone for a wrongful thing they did to us. Everyone has been verbally, emotionally, or physically hurt by someone in his or her life. But does this give us permission to repay the deed? No, we are not to repay evil for evil (see Rom. 12:17–21) but leave it in the hands of God.

Jesus said, "Blessed are the peacemakers, for they will be called sons of God" (Matt. 5:9). Because we belong to the one who created peace and we live a life of peace, we can become a peacemaker.

I read this anecdote that challenged me.

"Tell me the weight of a snowflake," a sparrow asked a wild dove.

"Nothing more than nothing," was the answer.

"In that case, I must tell you a marvelous story," the sparrow said. "I sat on the branch of a fir, close to its trunk, when it began to snow—not heavily, not in a raging blizzard—no, just like in a dream, without a sound, and without any violence. Since I did not have anything better to do, I counted the snowflakes settling on the twigs and needles of my branch. Their number was exactly 3,741,952. When the 3,741,953rd dropped onto the branch, nothing more than nothing, as you say, the branch broke off."

Having said that, the sparrow flew away.

The dove, since Noah's time an authority on the matter, thought about the story for a while, and finally said to herself, "Perhaps only one person's voice is lacking for peace to come to the world."[17]

YOU CAN MAKE A DIFFERENCE

Perhaps you're the voice that can bring peace to a troubled friend. You may be the one who can speak a peaceful solution to a situation that is tearing apart a marriage or a relationship between loved ones. You may hold the peaceful answer to a competitive, territorial, jealous force within your company or community. If you know the Peacemaker, he will produce within you the fruit of the Spirit called peace.

CHAPTER 4

PATIENCE

The Benefits of Waiting

I have never met a parent who didn't need great quantities of patience while raising his or her children. Husbands and wives also need to have patience with each other. Family members have to dig deep down inside to find more of this precious commodity when dealing with extended family. Employers and employees go through times when this attribute is one of the few things enabling them to work together. Although people can muster up patience by determination and hard work, God will help us develop patience that is beyond what most think is reasonable.

In *Fresh Wind, Fresh Fire,* Pastor Jim Cymbala of the Brooklyn Tabernacle speaks of an occasion when he desperately needed God's help. Jim and Carol's daughter Chrissy, although she had grown up in a solid Christian home, began living a reckless life. For two-and-a-half years she pulled away from her parents and God. Jim writes: "As the situation grew more serious, I tried everything. I begged, I pleaded, I scolded, I argued, I tried to control her with money. Looking back, I recognize the foolishness of my actions. Nothing worked; she just hardened more and more. Her boyfriend was everything we did not want for our child."[1]

Carol wondered if the family should leave New York as she was fearful her other children might head down the same path. After speaking to Chrissy, a minister friend said, "Jim, I love you and your wife, but the truth of the matter is, Chrissy's going to do what Chrissy's going to do. You don't really have much choice, now that she's eighteen. She's determined. You're going to have to accept whatever she decides." The only thing Jim and Carol could do was pray and try to show Chrissy love and patience.

One Tuesday night an unusual thing happened at Jim's church. During a prayer service, a member of his congregation asked if the church could stop everything and pray for Chrissy. Jim felt a little awkward asking for prayer for his own needs, as there were so many needs in the congregation; nevertheless, he was desperate. The church prayed sincerely, and Jim felt something happen. He had an assurance in his heart. Jim writes:

Thirty-two hours later, on Thursday morning, as I was shaving, Carol suddenly burst through the door, her eyes wide. "Go downstairs!" she blurted. "Chrissy's here."

"Chrissy's here?"

"Yes! Go down!"

"But Carol—I—"

"Just go down," she urged. "It's you she wants to see."

I wiped off the shaving foam and headed down the stairs, my heart pounding. As I came around the corner, I saw my daughter on the kitchen floor, rocking on her hands and knees, sobbing. Cautiously I spoke her name:

"Chrissy?"

She grabbed my pant leg and began pouring out her

anguish. "Daddy—Daddy—I've sinned against God. I've sinned against myself. I've sinned against you and Mommy. Please forgive me—"

Tears clouded my vision. I pulled her up from the floor and held her close as we cried together.

Suddenly she drew back. "Daddy," she said with a start, "who was praying for me? Who was praying for me?" Her voice was like that of a cross-examining attorney.

"What do you mean, Chrissy?"

"On Tuesday night, Daddy—who was praying for me?" I didn't say anything, so she continued:

"In the middle of the night, God woke me and showed me I was heading toward this abyss. There was no bottom to it—it scared me to death. I was so frightened. I realized how hard I've been, how wrong, how rebellious.

"But at the same time, it was like God wrapped his arms around me and held me tight. He kept me from sliding any farther as he said, 'I still love you.'

"Daddy, tell me the truth—who was praying for me Tuesday night?"

I looked into her bloodshot eyes, and once again I recognized the daughter we had raised."[2]

Chrissy did change. She attended a college where she prepared for a life of ministry and married an outstanding young man who became a pastor like his father-in-law. I can't say that patience changed Chrissy; most certainly it was the love of God and her decision to listen to his pleas to return to him. But there is no doubt that in the middle of this nightmare Jim and Carol needed supernatural patience. They needed to find a way to keep trusting, to keep waiting, to keep believing, and to keep their cool.

Have you ever been there?

When going through a difficult time, have you ever prayed, "Lord, please give me patience—now"? Developing patience takes time, and we all need as much patience as we can get.

Most have had the experience of driving home after a hard day's work, pulling onto the freeway, listening to some good music, perhaps even praying a little or thanking the Lord for a good day. Then all of a sudden someone sped by and swerved in front of your car (when there was no room) and you saw brake lights as they slowed down. The peaceful atmosphere in your car quickly became warm, and warm turned to hot. All of this took place in about fifteen seconds.

Or how about when you feel you are being treated unfairly by others? The boss just gave someone else the solid accounts and a raise. You have experienced this unfair treatment before, and now the boss has done it again. In frustration you put your papers in your briefcase and rush out of the office slamming the door (so that everyone else in the office can hear how angry you are).

Sometimes the washing machine breaks down, the water heater suddenly quits (in the middle of a shower), a tire goes flat while you are on the way to an important meeting, the kids won't stop yelling, or someone decides to tell you off over something you didn't do. Emotions can quickly shift from peaceful to angry, glad to mad, positive to negative because of the need for patience. As we walk through life, we all need God's help with our emotions and the way we choose to react. Thankfully, God supplies everything we need.

The Greek word for patience is *macrothumia*, which is a combination of two words, *macro* meaning "long" and *thumos* meaning "temper," and specifically points to the idea of anger taking a very long time to build before it is expressed. If and when it is ever expressed, it is under control.

Some people have "short tempers," which means they lose

their patience quickly and become angry. Little else in life is more uncomfortable or devastating than being a recipient of someone's temper release or uncontrolled anger. Often not much can be done to persuade them to "chill out." It seems that the more we try to persuade them to calm down, the angrier they become.

Others are able to control their temper and are patient with others. Even when they have the ability, and possibly the right, to react verbally, they exercise restraint. These people are *macrothumia* people. Patience, then, is a word meaning the opposite of inappropriate anger.

Gordon Fee writes in his book *God's Empowering Presence* that *macrothumia* is

> always used in contexts involving one's forbearance toward others. . . . Thus "longsuffering" has to do with one's long forbearance toward those who oppose or distress one in some way. Nowhere else does Paul attribute such forbearance to the direct working of the Spirit; but its appearance here shows that Spirit-empowering is not simply for joy and miracles but for this much-needed quality of "putting up with" those who need long and patient love and kindness.[3]

I believe God had a purpose in directing Paul to list the fruit of the Spirit in a certain order in Galatians 5:22–23. If we have love, joy, and peace in our lives, patience will be present also. The fruit all develop from one another, and all begin with love. J. I. Packer wrote in *Knowing and Doing the Will of God:*

> Love is the Christlike reaction to people's malice.
> Joy is the Christlike reaction to depressing circumstances.
> Peace is the Christlike reaction to troubles, threats, and
> invitations to anxiety.

Patience is the Christlike reaction to all that is maddening.

Kindness is the Christlike reaction to all that are unkind.

Goodness is the Christlike reaction to bad people and bad behavior.

Faithfulness and gentleness are the Christlike reactions to lies and fury.

Self-control is the Christlike reaction to every situation that goads you to lose your cool and hit out.[4]

So much of the fruit of the Spirit has to do with our reactions to people and to our circumstances in life. The fruit helps us choose what to do when situations or people seem not to be moving as quickly or acting as we would like them to.

When we are patient we do not quickly retaliate, "return like for like," or take revenge. Patience is self-restraint in the face of provocation. It doesn't quickly punish but thinks before it responds and, if it responds, it responds appropriately. People who have learned to let this fruit grow in their lives are able to "hang in there," to not surrender to circumstances or give up when going through trials.

GOD IS PATIENT WITH US

No one is more patient with us than God. I have often thought about his love and patience with me. It is hard to imagine the depth of God's patience in a world where people are overwhelmingly impatient with others and with their circumstances. The Bible tells us, "[God] is patient with you" (2 Peter 3:9). God is also patient with those you care about and, for that matter, with everyone.

When the Israelites were confessing their sins before God and acknowledging his greatness, the prophet Ezra prayed:

You alone are the LORD. You made the heavens, even the highest heavens, and all their starry host, the earth and all that is on it, the seas and all that is in them. You give life to everything, and the multitudes of heaven worship you.

You are the LORD God, who chose Abram and brought him out of Ur of the Chaldeans and named him Abraham. You found his heart faithful to you, and you made a covenant with him. . . . You have kept your promise because you are righteous.

You saw the suffering of our forefathers in Egypt; you heard their cry at the Red Sea. . . .

You divided the sea before them, so that they passed through it on dry ground, but you hurled their pursuers into the depths, like a stone into mighty waters. By day you led them with a pillar of cloud, and by night with a pillar of fire to give them light on the way they were to take.

You came down on Mount Sinai; you spoke to them from heaven. You gave them regulations and laws that are just and right, and decrees and commands that are good. . . . In their hunger you gave them bread from heaven and in their thirst you brought them water from the rock. . . .

But they, our forefathers, became arrogant and stiff-necked, and did not obey your commands. They refused to listen and failed to remember the miracles you performed among them. They became stiff-necked and in their rebellion appointed a leader in order to return to their slavery. But you are a forgiving God, gracious and compassionate, slow to anger and abounding in love. . . .

Because of your great compassion you did not abandon them in the desert. . . . For forty years you sustained them. . . .

They reveled in your great goodness. . . .

But as soon as they were at rest, they again did what was evil in your sight. . . .

For many years you were patient with them. . . . But in your great mercy you did not put an end to them or abandon them, for you are a gracious and merciful God. (Neh. 9:6–9, 11–13, 15–17, 19, 21, 25, 28, 30–31)

Throughout Scripture we see God expressing patience with people. In your life, marriage, temptation, or need, do not think for a moment that God has given up on you. Even if you are hard and tough on the outside, God knows that there is a silent yearning for his help. If you have given up on yourself, God hasn't. If you feel that you are out of strength to keep fighting, God will give you strength from a place you may not have expected. If you are continually trying to kick a habit and have run out of will, God can give you new determination. Even if you need to whisper, "God, I need your help," he will hear it as if you cried out. God will not walk out on you; don't walk out on him.

WE CAN GROW IN PATIENCE

In his book *The Life You've Always Wanted*, John Ortberg recalls some advice a friend gave him.

Not long after moving to Chicago, I called a wise friend to ask for some spiritual direction. I described the pace at which things tend to move in my current setting. I told him about the rhythms of our family life and about the present condition of my heart, as best I could discern it. What did I need to do, I asked him, to be spiritually healthy?

Long pause.

"You must ruthlessly eliminate hurry from your life," he said at last. Another long pause.

"Okay, I've written that one down," I told him, a little impatiently. "That's a good one. Now what else is there?" I had many things to do, and this was a long-distance conversation, so I was anxious to cram as many units of spiritual wisdom into the least amount of time possible.

Another long pause.

"There is nothing else," he said.

He is the wisest spiritual mentor I have known. And while he doesn't know every detail about every grain of sin in my life, he knows quite a bit. And from an immense quiver of spiritual sagacity, he drew only one arrow. "There is nothing else," he said. "You must ruthlessly eliminate hurry from your life."[5]

Ortberg then comments, "Imagine for a moment that someone gave you this prescription, with the warning that your life depends on it. Consider the possibility that perhaps your life does depend on it. Hurry is the great enemy of spiritual life in our day. Hurry can destroy our souls. Hurry can keep us from living well. As Carl Jung wrote, 'Hurry is not of the devil; hurry is the devil.'"[6]

I think most of us can relate to Ortberg's dilemma. How do we slow down, pace ourselves, or control the tyranny of the urgent? If we are not careful, the enemy of our souls can rob us of peace as we frantically sprint through life. We Americans are often guilty of what psychologists call "polyphasic activity," or doing multiple things at the same time. As we drive to work, we talk on the telephone, drink our coffee, eat our donut, look over our daytimer, and catch the news on the radio. While pretending to listen to our spouse or children, we watch the news, eat dinner, look over the paper, and try to unwind from our polyphasic day. Wow! It's no wonder stress, depression, and anxiety are major mental health problems in our day.

God is not in a hurry—he has everything under control. He

is not frantically rushing around full of nervous energy trying to accomplish his goals. He is patient with us, and patience can be a controlling factor in our lives as well. Patience will develop naturally as we grow in Christ and depend on the Holy Spirit, because we are part of the one who is patience.

As we avoid sin and sincerely desire to be led by the Spirit, we will experience steady growth in patience. We will become less angry (or hostile) and have more control over what we say. Our life will seem calmer. When we find it necessary to respond assertively or to appropriately confront someone, we will be in control. The Holy Spirit will help us with our sense of timing as we determine when (or if) we need to say or do something. This maturity doesn't come overnight; God will help us develop new habits as we grow in our relationship with him.

When people are impatient or angry, they may choose to deal with their anger in any of a number of ways. Some *repress* it by stuffing it down. Over the long run this can cause bitterness, deep anguish, resentment, and even physical problems. Some *suppress* it by being sarcastic or projecting negative feelings or anger onto another person or object. Some *express* it in a negative way through violent reactions, fits of rage, uncontrolled outbursts, verbal abuse, revenge, or worse. These negative ways of expressing anger will only hurt others as well as the angry person.

According to the Associated Press, in 1994 hospital emergency rooms in the United States treated 1.4 million victims of violence or suspected violence. The Justice Department analyzed the data and reported in 1997 that roughly half of these victims were hurt by someone they knew. Seventeen percent of the victims were injured by a spouse, former spouse, or a current or former boyfriend or girlfriend. A relative such as a parent or child injured 8 percent of the victims. Friends or acquaintances hurt 23 percent.[7]

Incidents of "road rage," those horrible crimes in which someone gets angry in traffic and attempts to harm another driver, are increasing all over the country. A recent story from the *Philadelphia Daily News* stated that aggressive driving accounted for half of their city's auto accidents. A survey of accidents during the 1990s showed that four of the top six causes for accidents were not carelessness but aggression: running stoplights, tailgating, improper turning, and failure to heed a stopped vehicle. Aggressive drivers, the paper concluded, kill two to four times more people than drunks do.[8]

Between January 1, 1990, and September 1, 1996, a total of 12,828 people were injured or killed as a result of aggressive driving, including ninety-four children under the age of fifteen.[9]

We have grown accustomed to hearing about out-of-control people on the evening news. But God has a better way for us to deal with our disappointments, frustrations, and difficulties. One healthy way to deal with anger is to express it positively. Talk the problem through or take practical steps to prevent more conflict in the future. Go on a long walk, play racquetball, count to one hundred (or one thousand!), do something to get away from the situation for a while. Many have found that journaling can also bring relief as they can express their anger on paper. Writing relieves the emotional pressure, and what we write never has to be shown to anyone.

Another positive way to deal with anger is to confess it to God. Admit to God that you are angry and ask him for solutions to the problem. Be open to his leading in your efforts to understand the person and discover ways to reconcile with him or her.

Impatience and destructive anger is largely a learned response; however, it can be replaced with an appropriate and loving response that is under the control of the Holy Spirit. Proverbs tells us that "a patient man calms a quarrel" (15:18). And Paul reminds us to "be patient with everyone" (1 Thess. 5:14).

IMPATIENCE OFTEN COMES BECAUSE OF FAULTY OR INAPPROPRIATE GOALS

Although we cannot depend on our emotions to be *up* every day and should not base our commitments on how we *feel*, we need to listen to our emotions, for they are a gift from God. If we are feeling anxious or angry or are struggling with depression, it could be because we have made goals in our lives that are not wise. Any goal that can be blocked by forces out of your control is not a healthy goal, because the success you desire in meeting that goal is out of your hands. It becomes a recipe for stress.

Some of us are perfectionists, and we simply cannot quit until we think the project is done or the goal has been perfectly met. Perfectionists tend to think they have the right to always reach their optimum goal. Extremely high standards in almost everything drive them, and they are dissatisfied with anything less. When their standards are not reached, they often become angry with themselves or someone else. Hard work and diligence are good qualities; however, if we are perfectionists, we will be frustrated, dissatisfied, and impatient because there is always more to do. We need to find a point of closure in our efforts to do an excellent job.

For those who constantly hold on to their *rights*, I came across this definition of patience: "Patience is an excellent conscious defense against the frequent minor frustrations of life. Selfish, immature individuals who give themselves too many rights are constantly plagued with anger, since so many of their 'rights' are violated. Giving up those rights to God and expecting fewer things to be perfect will result in patience, greater humility, less anger, and greater joy in life."[10]

Our goals may be good, for example, raising our children to mature into godly, successful leaders. Although we pray and work hard to encourage them, influence them, educate them, and help them in every possible way, when they are adults they will make their own decisions. If they decide to walk away from the ways we have worked to develop in their lives, we can end up blaming ourselves, others, and even God. But we simply cannot control outside circumstances or people. Although we can control some factors, people will do what they want to do.

Emotions such as anger, anxiety, and depression are often present because something is not going the way we want it to go. What do we do? Someone said, "Do your best and trust God with the rest." We can have wonderful, honorable desires and work hard to achieve them, but if we can't achieve them, we need to leave them in God's hands. This is where patience is necessary. We need to find a place of rest and trust God to work out his perfect will.

WE ARE TO BE PATIENT WITH OTHERS

Even though Moses knew that God was a patient God, he as a leader was sometimes annoyed with the Israelites because of their disobedience toward God or their lack of trust in him. Thus he sometimes became angry with them when they complained about God's provisions and failed to trust God (see Num. 20:10–11). So when God told Moses to speak to the rock to get water for the people, Moses instead struck the rock out of anger. His impatience caused him to disobey God, and because of that, he was not permitted to enter the Promised Land with the Israelites. Moses was normally a patient person, but even patient people have their limits. Everyone needs God's supernatural assistance in this area, because sooner or later we will reach our limit with someone or something.

It is helpful to try to see others as Jesus sees them. We may wonder:

Why are they acting the way they are? It could be because of tremendous pain or loss in their lives.

Why do they seem so arrogant, distant, or unwilling to develop a friendship? It could be that they are protecting themselves from rejection.

Why does their heart seem so hard toward the things of God? It could be that they have had an incredible loss and they are blaming God.

Our patience and understanding can be used by the Holy Spirit to help others. William Law wrote,

> We may take for a certain rule, that the more the divine nature and life of Jesus is manifest in us, and the higher our sense of righteousness and virtue, the more we shall pity and love those who are suffering from the blindness, disease, and death of sin. The sight of such people then, instead of raising in us a haughty contempt or holier-than-thou indignation, will rather fill us with such tenderness and compassion as when we see the miseries of a dread disease."[11]

The only way we can truly be patient with others is to see them through the eyes of Jesus. Observing devastating, horrible, discourteous, evil ways that people treat people will often harden our hearts toward others. Christ sees right through outward appearances and understands their need.

Husbands and Wives Are to Be Patient with Each Other

Paul instructs husbands not to be harsh with their wives and to love them as Christ loves the church (Col. 3:19). Peter instructs husbands to be considerate of the needs of their wives "so that nothing will hinder your prayers" (1 Peter 3:7). Wives are to respect their husbands and submit to them (see Eph. 5:22, 33; Col. 3:18).

All of these instructions for the marital relationship involve patience. One of the reasons men are harsh is impatience. When things do not go as a man feels they should, or when things are not moving along quickly, he may become impatient and, as a result, harsh. For a husband to have understanding, he must listen and take time to find out what his wife's needs are.

A wife needs patience to respect her husband and submit to his role in the family. She needs patience with him as he matures, becomes more sensitive to her needs, acquires knowledge and skill as a father, develops expertise in his career, and most of all, becomes more Christlike. Submission to his God-given role is a demonstration of trust in God's will and plan for the ideal family. The marriage relationship itself, in virtually all areas (from finances to discipline of children), requires patience and commitment.

Raising Children Takes Tremendous Patience

We usually figure this out after they are in our home for about two days! In his excellent book *Parenting Isn't for Cowards*, James Dobson wrote,

> One thing is clear to me; behavioral scientists have been far too simplistic in their explanation of human behavior. We are more than the aggregate of our experiences. We are more than the quality of our nutrition. We are more than our genetic heritage. We are more than our biochemistry. And certainly, we are more than our parents' influence. God has created us as unique individuals, capable of independent and rational thought that is not attributable to any source. That is what makes the task of

parenting so challenging and rewarding. Just when you think you have your kids figured out, you had better brace yourself! Something new is coming your way.[12]

Parents need to know how to properly discipline their children and how to be patient with them, or else they may overwhelm their children with frustration. Paul instructs, "Fathers do not embitter your children, or they will become discouraged" (Col. 3:21). Some parents are impatient and lack understanding of how their children feel. Sometimes parents force their children to mature too quickly or to find their "niche in life" too soon. They often push and demand and treat their children unfairly, provoking them to anger and rebellion. Again Paul instructs fathers not to "exasperate your children" (Eph. 6:4).

You Are to Be Patient with People Who Do Not Know Christ

The fruit of patience is not just applicable to the way you treat Christians but to people in general. People who work with you, live near you, or see you in public should see the attribute of patience exemplified in your life. Your patience will make you seem different from those who do not know Christ. Non-Christians will want to know how you developed this quality. If God is patient with those who do not know Christ, "not wanting any to perish," we can be patient with them as well.

We Are to Be Patient with Ourselves

I like the advice of St. Francis de Sales: "Have patience with all things, but chiefly have patience with yourself. Do not lose courage in considering your imperfections, but instantly set about remedying them—every day begin the task anew."[13]

Paul wrote, "Brothers, I do not consider myself yet to have

taken hold of it. But one thing I do: Forgetting what is behind and straining toward what is ahead, I press on toward the goal to win the prize for which God has called me heavenward in Christ Jesus" (Phil. 3:13–14). All of us need determination to keep our eternal focus, because daily distractions, temptations, worries, riches, and evil desires can paralyze our commitment to continue growing in Christ. Not getting over past mistakes, failures, and sins can be an unnecessary weight that will persistently trouble us. We need to go to Christ daily to seek his will, ask for forgiveness of sin, and determine that we will glorify him in all we say and do.

In his classic book *The Imitation of Christ*, Thomas à Kempis wrote,

> Patience is necessary in this life because so much of life is fraught with adversity. No matter how hard we try, our lives will never be without strife and grief. Thus, we should not strive for peace that is without temptation, or for a life that never feels adversity. Peace is not found by escaping temptations, but by being tried by them. We will have discovered peace when we have been tried and come through the trial of temptation.[14]

We all are in a growing mode; none of us has arrived. But growing requires discipline and commitment. We must learn to keep our eyes focused on Jesus and on our eternal reward. If your past troubles you, choose to act and speak differently—today.

Patience is something with which we could all use improvement. The Holy Spirit within us desires to develop the same kind of patience God has. The incredible patience he has with us is the kind of patience he wants us to have with one another. Thus it cannot be separated from love. It is a supernatural work of his Spirit when we try to understand why people act the way they do and then respond to their behavior with love, truth, and proper timing instead of hastily or with uncontrolled anger. Walking in the Spirit means that we listen to God and follow his instructions as we encounter various challenges throughout our day. When we consistently walk in God's Spirit, God's character will find expression in our lives.

Senate chaplain Lloyd Ogilvie writes,

Perhaps our problem with impatience is that we misunderstand patience. It is not acquiescence, or perpetual placidity, or feckless lack of fiber. Patience must be rooted in an overarching confidence that there is someone in control of the universe, or world, and our life. We need to know that God does work things together for good for those who love Him. A patient person knows the shortness of time and the length of eternity. Patience is really faith in action. No wonder it is called an aspect of the fruit of the Spirit. It is one of the matchless characteristics of Christ himself. If we would learn patience, He alone can teach us. There are many facsimiles of virtue, but authentic patience comes as a result of our deep personal relationship with Christ.[15]

CHAPTER 5

KINDNESS

Reaching Out to Others

Robert De Vincenzo, the great Argentine golfer, once won a tournament and, after receiving the check and smiling for the cameras, went to the clubhouse and prepared to leave. He walked alone to his car in the parking lot and was approached by a young woman. She congratulated him on his victory and then told him that her child was seriously ill and near death. She did not know how she could pay the doctor's bill and hospital expenses.

De Vincenzo was touched by her story, and he took out a pen and endorsed his winning check to the woman. "Make some good days for the baby," he said as he pressed the check into her hand.

The next week he was having lunch at a country club when a Professional Golf Association official came to his table. "Some of the boys told me you met a young woman in the parking lot last week after you won that tournament." De Vincenzo nodded. "Well," said the official, "I have news for you. She's a phony. She has no sick baby. She's not even married. She fleeced you, my friend."

"You mean there is no baby who is dying?" queried De Vincenzo.

"That's right," answered the official.

"That's the best news I've heard all week," De Vincenzo replied.[1]

Although this story is not necessarily about a Christian's treatment of a person in need, it most certainly demonstrates the kind of attitude Christians should have. We should be concerned for the welfare of others and do all we can to be kind to them even if we are taken advantage of. The fact that there is potential for people to use us or be dishonest with us must not prevent us from doing acts of kindness. We are to see deeper than the potential for manipulation and deceit. We must see their need. Even concerning our enemies, Jesus said, "Do good to them, and lend to them without expecting to get anything back. Then your reward will be great, and you will be sons of the Most High, because he is kind to the ungrateful and wicked" (Luke 6:35–36).

God is kind. He said through Jeremiah, "I am the LORD, who exercises kindness . . ." (Jer. 9:24). The psalmist said, "You are forgiving and good, O LORD" (Ps. 86:5). Luke tells us that those who imitate God in being kind to the ungrateful and wicked "will be sons of the Most High" (Luke 6:35).

God's kindness to sinners is designed to lead them to repentance (Rom. 2:4). His kindness to believers should encourage us to continue in his kindness (Rom. 11:22) by treating others as he has treated us (Eph. 4:32), for love is not only patient, it is kind (see 1 Cor. 13:4).

Hudson Taylor, famous missionary to China and founder of the China Inland Mission, was asked to go to the home of a very poor woman and pray for her because she was ill. During that time many other religious leaders charged people money for such service, but the woman's family knew Hudson would not charge.

When he began to pray for her he felt uncomfortable because he had a coin in his pocket that he knew would help her in her poverty. As he knelt to pray he hesitated, thinking that he should give her the coin. Yet he rationalized that he had only enough food in his own home for two more meals. He needed the money too. When the conviction didn't go away he decided to give the woman his coin. As he knelt in prayer for her healing he felt great freedom and encouragement.[2] Taylor's example teaches us that we should seldom repress an urge to be kind.

The fruit of the Spirit is more than an attitude or a trait that we desire; it is evidence that the Holy Spirit lives in us. Some people have thought that the Holy Spirit is mystical, spooky, or unapproachable, but these are not true perceptions. The Holy Spirit is love, joy, peace, patience, kindness, goodness, faithfulness, gentleness, and self-control. He is very approachable and desires that we listen to him, be like him, and walk in him. God's purpose in having the Holy Spirit dwell within believers is that we might depend on him to direct our lives and illustrate God's personality to others.

The Greek word for kindness is *chrestos*. Jack Hayford describes this portion of the Holy Spirit's fruit as "goodness in action, sweetness of disposition, gentleness in dealing with others, benevolence, kindness, affability. The word describes the ability to act for the welfare of those taxing your patience. The Holy Spirit removes abrasive qualities from the character of one under His control."[3]

As you walk through your day, are you concerned about listening to the voice of the Holy Spirit as he prompts you to be kind to your family members, neighbors, coworkers, and all others with whom you come in contact? As Christians we are to be known as *chrestos* people. Those who know us should be able to testify that we are kind.

A PARABLE OF KINDNESS

In Jesus' story of the good Samaritan he points out three charac-teristics of kindness: it is compassionate, it takes action, and it is powerful.

> A man was going down from Jerusalem to Jericho, when he fell into the hands of robbers. They stripped him of his clothes, beat him and went away, leaving him half dead. A priest happened to be going down the same road, and when he saw the man he passed by on the other side. So too, a Levite, when he came to the place and saw him, passed by on the other side. But a Samaritan, as he traveled, came where the man was; and when he saw him, he took pity on him. He went to him and bandaged his wounds, pouring on oil and wine. Then he put the man on his own don-key, took him to an inn and took care of him. The next day he took out two silver coins and gave them to the innkeeper. "Look after him," he said, "and when I return, I will reimburse you for any extra expense you may have." (Luke 10:30–35)

Kindness Is Full of Compassion

On my (Wayde's) way to the office during rush hour I noticed a Ford Pinto with a flat tire parked on the edge of the freeway. A woman stood staring at her tire in frustration while several small children sat in the car. I sped by just glancing at her dilemma but immediately thought about the potential danger of her situation. My schedule was tight, but I thought someone needed to help her. Quickly I pulled over to the side and carefully backed my car up to hers. She was nervous, almost in tears, and frightened about the heavy traffic.

I asked her if I could change her tire. She said, "Please, would you? I'm not sure how all of this works."

I said, "Let's get the kids out of the car and onto the grassy area,"

It took about ten minutes to do the job. With gratitude she loaded the children back into the car and drove off. That week during a brief testimony time in the Wednesday night Bible study at church, I noticed that the lady I had helped stood up to thank God for a man who had changed her tire. She felt that God had answered her prayer.

How do we respond when we see people in need? As Christians we are to be full of *kind* compassion, an emotion that will move us to the very depths of our being. Simply put, a kind person cares about people.

The Samaritan "saw" the wounded man. This parable is an illustration of how Jesus sees people. In the middle of a crowd of hungry, tired people, Jesus heard the cry of a leprous man (Mark 1:41). When Jesus looked at a busy city full of people going in a thousand directions, he saw them as harassed, helpless sheep without a caring shepherd, and he felt compassion for them (Matt. 9:36). When he saw the funeral procession of the son of the widow of Nain, he was moved by her tremendous sorrow (Luke 7:13). Jesus was not detached, distant, or indifferent to the pain he saw in people's lives. People were not a hindrance, a nuisance, or a bother to him; rather, he saw their need as an opportunity to help.

Eusebius writes of Jesus in the same words (whether intentionally or not we do not know) that were used to describe Hippocrates, the founder of Greek medicine: "He was like some excellent physician, who, in order to cure the sick, examines what is repulsive, handles sores, and reaps pain himself from the sufferings of others. Jesus never regarded the sufferer with indifference, still less with loathing and disgust. He regarded the sufferer and the needy with a pity which issued in help."[4]

Perhaps you have wondered how some can be aware of

incredible need and then look the other way. The answer is, we can choose to not feel, to not be compassionate. During the time Jesus told the good Samaritan story, the Stoics were the highest thinkers of the day. One of their ideas was that they needed to be cautious about how much they felt another's pain. They taught that if a man could "feel either sorrow or joy, it means that someone else can bring sorrow or joy to him. That is to say, it means that someone else can affect him. Now, if someone else can affect him, can alter his feelings, can make him happy or sad, it means that that person has power over him, and is therefore, for the moment at least, greater than he."[5]

This reminds me of a twenty-first-century Pharisee who explained why Christians become ill. He used the following illustration:

Suppose a salesman arrives at your door with a bag of rattlesnakes. If you are stupid enough to let him in, then don't complain when you get bit. In like manner, "this person asserts," the devil arrives at your door with a bag of sicknesses and misfortunes. If you don't have enough faith or if there is sin in your life, you let him in with his contents. Why should anyone feel kindness toward you for being such a faithless person![6]

This Pharisee would likely leave you lying on the side of the road and perhaps give you a lecture about claiming your healing.

I am also reminded of the husband who will not help his wife when she needs advice and counsel because of a "worse than best" decision she has made, and of the wife who will not assist and encourage her husband when he is discouraged about his career. It is mean to think that way, and it simply is not the way God treats his children. God helps us even when we have brought trouble on ourselves. We are to do likewise.

In an innovative study, a group of students at Princeton Theological Seminary were asked to prepare a short speech or lecture that they would deliver at another building on campus. Some of the students were assigned the parable of the good Samaritan; others were to speak on the occupational interests of those who go to seminary. Preparation time was short, some students having only the few minutes it took to walk between the two buildings to decide what they would say. Others were given a little more time before they were to make their presentation. The researchers (Darley and Batson, 1973) used the path between the buildings as their own version of the road from Jerusalem to Jericho. Beside the path they placed a shabbily dressed person slumped over with his eyes closed, coughing and groaning. Which seminarians would help the "victim"? Would the topic to be addressed make a difference? Would time constraints be a factor?

The results showed that it made no difference what the talk was about. "Indeed, on several occasions, a seminary student going to give his talk on the parable of the good Samaritan literally stepped over the victim as he hurried on his way (p. 107). How much time the student had, though, was important. Those who were told they were already late were significantly less apt to offer aid than those who were not so rushed."[7]

In his parable who did Jesus say walked by the man in need and why? William Barclay wrote in his commentary on Luke,

- There was the priest. He hastened past. No doubt he was remembering that he who touched a dead man was unclean for seven days (Num. 19:11). He could not be sure but he feared that the man was dead; to touch him would mean losing his turn of duty in the Temple; and he refused to risk that. He set the claims of ceremony above those of charity. The Temple and its liturgy meant more to him than the pain of man.

- There was the Levite. He seems to have gone nearer to the man before he passed on. The bandits were in the habit of using decoys. One of their number would act the part of a wounded man; and when some unsuspecting traveler stopped over him, the others would rush upon him and overpower him. The Levite was a man whose motto was, "Safety first." He would take no risks to help anyone.[8]

The third person who walked by the injured man was the Samaritan. Luke tells us that "when he saw him, he took pity on him" (Luke 10:33). The difference between the two religious leaders and the Samaritan was that when the priest and the Levite saw the man they wondered, *What will happen to us if we help him?* while the Samaritan thought, *What will happen to the man, if I don't help him?*

The Bible instructs us to "be kind and compassionate to one another" (Eph. 4:32). When we see people in need we feel compassion, and compassion will motivate us to do something.

Kindness Takes Action

Seeing the needs of others will often give us ideas about something kind we can do. The good Samaritan not only had compassion for the injured traveler, he decided to do everything he could to assist the man.

We need to understand that the Samaritan took a great risk when he chose to stop and help the man. Barclay explains,

The road from Jerusalem to Jericho was a notoriously dangerous road. Jerusalem is 2,300 feet above sea level; the Dead Sea, near which Jericho stood, is 1,300 feet below sea level. So then, in somewhat less than twenty miles, this road dropped 3,600 feet, It was a road of narrow, rocky defiles, and of sudden turnings which made it the happy hunting ground of brigands. In the fifth century Jerome tells us that it was still called "The Red, or Bloody Way." In the nineteenth century it was still necessary to pay safety money to the local Sheiks before one could travel on it. As late as the early 1930s H. V. Morton tells us that he was warned to get home before dark, if he intended to use the road, because a certain Abu Jildah was adept at holding up cars and robbing travelers and tourists, and escaping to the hills before the police could arrive. When Jesus told this story, he was telling about the kind of thing that was constantly happening on the Jerusalem to Jericho road.[9]

This road reminds me of numerous places in America—inner cities, drug-infested neighborhoods, places where drive-by shootings happen, communities where people put bars on their windows and doors. These places are full of people who are in pain. Many are crying out for help because they fear being wounded or have been wounded.

Not long ago my wife and I (Wayde) visited the Dream Center, a church and ministry program located in a rough area of North Hollywood. I was asked to speak in the midweek service on a Thursday night. I'll never forget that night.

Driving up to the building—a huge old hospital—amazed me. Parked outside were Harley Davidson motorcycles—not the kind you see in some middle-class businessman's driveway, but the kind you see in a group of Hell's Angels. Just inside the building was the proof. We saw dozens of bikers with tattoos, muscle shirts, missing teeth, and scars on their arms and faces. This was quite a sight, especially in church. They greeted us warmly although we were dressed very differently. They grabbed our hands, hugged our necks, and welcomed us to the Dream Center. That night we were introduced to ex-prostitutes, ex-drug addicts, ex-street people, and a few others who were still involved in destructive behavior. We also met people who had made a lot of money through their involvement in the Hollywood scene. The room was packed with people who wanted to worship God and hear from his Word. They knew that God had a "dream" for all of their lives; he offered salvation, peace, contentment, security, and health to all.

The Dream Center is pastored by a young, blond, faithful and talented man named Matthew Barnett. He could have gone almost anywhere in ministry, but he chose a place most of us wouldn't go near. Why? Because he heard a cry for help. He saw wounded, broken, devastated people who needed a shepherd, and he took the risk of personal injury. He was so deeply moved by the need that he decided to do something about it.

Paul wrote, "As God's chosen people, holy and dearly loved, clothe yourselves with compassion, kindness, humility, gentleness and patience" (Col 3:12). Kindness, like the other fruit of the Spirit, is something we put on daily, like our clothing. Not only is this something that God will encourage us to do because we are connected to the Vine, it is a deliberate personal decision.

The good Samaritan went to the wounded man, talked to him, bandaged him, and took him to a place where he could rest and heal. Compassion without action is worthless. Like faith without works, it is dead. We must do something to make a difference.

Both you and I know of people or situations that could use our kindness. First on our agenda should be our families. Kindness is best learned and developed in the home with our spouse and children. If you have been married for even just a short time or have children, you know that family members have difficult times. If your spouse is hurt, depressed, or confused, you have an opportunity to exhibit great kindness. Over the years, both Wayde and I have counseled hundreds of couples. A common statement from wives is, "He is kind to me only when he wants something." Usually that has to do with a new toy (boat or extra car they cannot afford, etc.) or something physical. I have often thought that if kindness were something both husbands and wives focused on daily, many marriages would be saved.

Your child may be feeling insecure or scared, may be doing poorly in school, or may even be in jail because of a stupid decision. This is the time to demonstrate kindness and not a time to distance yourself. We must be ready to help our family members when they need us. When we develop a lifestyle of showing kindness in our homes, we will be more apt to consider ways to show kindness to those in our church, community, and workplace.

Kindness Is Powerful

In our dog-eat-dog, competitive world many people view kindness as a weakness. Those who demonstrate kindness swim against the stream of callousness and insensitivity. They stop to investigate when they see a need, even though most others would walk on by. When they think of an idea that may help someone else, they tell that person about it. They have an assurance that God is keeping score.

When Paul wrote to Timothy about the characteristics of godly leaders, he said, "The Lord's servant must not quarrel; instead, he must be kind to everyone" (2 Tim. 2:24). No matter how powerful a person's preaching, how large his or her ministry, or how popular he or she might be, without kindness that person is not much of a spiritual leader.

Kind people are sensitive to others' needs. Philippians 2:4 tells us we "should look not only to our own interests, but also to the interests of others." Sensitivity is a tremendous strength that we can develop. We all have people around us who are hurting. We are to be sensitive to their pain and endeavor to assist them, listen to them, pray for them, and just be there for them when they need us.

Kind people look for opportunities to encourage others. When Paul (formerly Saul) gave his life to Christ (Acts 9) many believers were still afraid of him because he had persecuted Christians. The disciples resisted him when he tried to join them. Barnabas, however, saw what God had done in Paul's life and knew that he had truly become a Christian. Barnabas made an effort to explain Paul's salvation experience to the apostles and told them how Paul now preached powerfully in the name of Jesus. Because of Barnabas's support, Paul was accepted and trusted. I've often thought, *Where would Paul be without Barnabas?* Barnabas lived up to his name, which means "son of encouragement."

People all around us need our support. Your encouragement may be the thing that motivates them to do the right thing, not give up, or hold on a little longer. Proverbs 15:4 says, "The tongue that brings healing is a tree of life, but a deceitful tongue crushes the spirit." Some people look for opportunities to say something nice, kind, and truthful. They are healing. Others are rude and insensitive to others. They crush people's spirits.

Kind people tell the truth. Sometimes the greatest act of kindness may be to help someone understand a fault or wrong behavior to which he or she may be blind. We "shoot straight" with people while packaging our words with love, kindness, and mercy. Proverbs 27:6 tells us that "wounds from a friend can be trusted, but an enemy multiplies kisses."

I'm grateful that my doctor is a Christian. He is faithful to his church, is a good husband and father, and is extremely conscientious in his work. I am also grateful that he tells me the truth. If he only talked to me about the Lord, his family, or how much he loves his work, I would feel that he was missing something. However, he also tells me the truth about my health, If he suspects something needs attention, he speaks to me about it and may request further tests or refer me to a specialist to double-check his thinking. He doesn't try to make me feel good by always saying, "Everything's great!" If he told me that everything was great when it wasn't, it could cost me my life! Likewise, we need to be truthful with others and we need others around us who will speak truth into our lives in a loving way.

Kind people care enough to confront or rebuke a brother or sister in Christ when necessary. It would be unkind to ignore another Christian's behavior that could injure them or someone else physically, emotionally, or spiritually. At times people have said to me, "I'll lose them as a friend if I speak to them about their harmful behavior." It is better to lose a friendship than to keep quiet and watch the other person get hurt. This takes real strength. We must do what is kind and right and not let their rejection of us influence how much we care about them.

Kindness isn't always giving people what they want, because what they want may bring harm to them. For example, you would cause great difficulty for your children if every time they wanted something you gave it to them. As children grow older it is absolutely necessary that they develop maturity, and with that comes the reality of having to work for a living and for the things they desire. If they never learn that truth, they will likely limp through life.

Kind people look for opportunities to show kindness. David wrote in the Twenty-Third Psalm, "Surely goodness and love will follow me all the days of my life" (v. 6). In the original language the words "follow me," mean that God's goodness, mercy, and love will pursue me and hunt me down all of my life. God, our Father, is constantly looking for ways to help us, to bless us, and to care for us. He is always ready to give us counsel. He is never too busy and loves to take time for us. His kindness is everlasting toward you and me. As God's children we are to be like him.

Jill Briscoe writes in her book *Running on Empty,*

I had been traveling for two weeks straight, speaking at meetings. Somehow the tight schedule allowed only time for talking and not much for eating! Whenever it was mealtime, I found myself on one more airplane. On this particular day it was hot, it was summer, and I was tired and hungry. My flight had been delayed, and by the time I arrived at the next conference center, I discovered that my hosts had gone to bed. (In the morning I learned that because of the delayed flight, they presumed I would not be coming until the following day—hence, no welcoming committee.) I wandered around the large dining room, hoping to find something to eat, but all the doors into the kitchen had been locked. "Lord," I prayed, "I really don't care what I eat, but I need something—while I'm talking to you about this, I've got a yearning for peaches! Oh, for a lovely, refreshing, juicy peach!" Then I smiled. That was just the sort of prayer I counseled others against offering! I sighed, picked up my bags, and went to my assigned cabin.

When I arrived at my room . . . a basket of peaches sat on the doorstep smiling up at me! I lifted them up and felt my loving Lord's smile. (It could have been oranges and apples, you know!) Never before or since have I received a whole basket of delicious, fresh peaches. . . . The Lord provided a sweet touch that reminded me of his great love.[10]

We have numerous opportunities to be kind to people. Look for these times and follow your inclinations. In his book *Lines above Tintern Abbey*, William Wordsworth rightly said, "That best portion of a good man's life, His little, nameless, unremembered acts/Of kindness and love."[11] Think about it for a moment. Who around you could use your help, encouragement, or a little of your time?

Although the good Samaritan probably had a schedule and

plans like those who passed by the injured man, he didn't do what they did. He let his schedule be interrupted. Most likely, kindness was a regular part of his life. This kind act was probably not the exception but the rule. The Holy Spirit wants each of us to make a habit of being kind.

BEGIN TO LISTEN AND RESPOND TODAY

Set aside this book for a moment and ask God to help you be kind. Who comes to your mind? What kind of activity do you sense you should be involved in to demonstrate kindness to someone? Is the "someone" in your family? Your office? Your church? Your neighborhood?

God is kind, and his Spirit dwells in your life. He constantly urges you to forgive those who have hurt you, taken advantage of you, or rejected you. Look deeper than their mistreatment and be kind anyway. Don't dwell on how they have hurt you; look deeper and understand that God loves them and wants to show his kindness to them through you. His kindness and mercy could come through your decision to do a good deed or to change your attitude toward them. Ask God to help you forgive them and to be kind to them. He will help you.

CHAPTER 6

GOODNESS

Learning to Live Generously

The Southern California radio announcer kept listeners aware that a flower was about to bloom.

I thought, *Why all this fuss over a flower?* I love flowers, but announcing the blooming of a flower on the news seemed a little extreme.

But not for this flower! I'd never heard of anything like this before. The flower, native to Indonesia, was billed as the world's largest and could grow more than six feet tall. It had bloomed previously only nine times in the twentieth century, and any day bloom number ten was about to appear. People flocked into Huntington Library's Art Collections and Botanical Gardens to watch and smell. The expectation of many who enjoy smelling flowers may have been "the larger the flower the better the fragrance." This flower, however, had the unusual distinction of being the world's stinkiest. A vile scent is emitted when it fully blooms.

Claudia Puig reported on the giant flower in *USA Today*, "The flower is distantly related to the calla lily, but it looks more like something out of *Little Shop of Horrors*, It emits an odor that smells like rotting flesh, hence its Indonesian name *bunga bangkai*, or corpse flower,"[1] Kathy Musical, the library's plant collection curator, explained, "The fetid stench is to attract pollinators. It smells like a dead animal to attract dung beetles and carrion beetles. They crawl into the flower and pollinate it. Ain't nature grand?"[2]

This flower reminds me of some people. Though they may appear bigger than life because of their financial success, societal status, material possessions, or educational development, when you get near them they surprise you by emitting a bad attitude, compromising lifestyle, or hardness toward others. What you discover when you begin to know them is different from what seems apparent at a distance. Their "stench" makes you want to run away from them as quickly as you can.

The fruit of the Spirit, on the other hand, has incredible drawing power. Though some of us believers may not be particularly attractive, these incredible, God-given attributes make people want to be around us. Whether we are tall, short, wide, thin, rich, poor, famous, or unknown, our godly fruit is a pleasant surprise to those around us.

WHO IS GOOD?

Good is the absence of defect or flaw and the presence of complete wholesomeness. Jesus said that only God is good. When Jesus was called "good teacher," he responded by saying, "Why do you call me good? No one is good—except God alone" (Mark 10:17–18). Jesus was not denying his deity, but he quickly challenged the man to think about what he was saying, "Sir, do you understand what you are saying when you call me good? Because only God is good."

Agathosune, the Greek word translated "goodness," is a rare word that combines being good and doing good.[3] It means kindness in actual manifestation, virtue equipped for action, a bountiful propensity both to will and do what is good, intrinsic goodness producing generosity, and godlike state or being.

Concerning goodness, Billy Graham writes,

> The word "good" in the language of Scripture literally means "to be like God," because He alone is the One who is perfectly good. It is one thing, however, to have high ethical standards but quite another for the Holy Spirit to produce the goodness that has its depths in the Godhead. The meaning here is more than just "doing good." Goodness goes far deeper. Goodness is love in action. It carries with it not only the idea of righteousness imputed, but righteousness demonstrated in everyday living by the Holy Spirit. It is doing good out of a good heart, to please God, without expecting medals and rewards. Christ wants this kind of goodness to be the way of life for every Christian.[4]

"Goodness," a word used twenty times in the Bible, describes moral or ethical character. Paul commended the church in Rome by saying, "I myself am convinced, my brothers, that you yourselves are full of goodness" (Rom. 15:14). When instructing the Ephesian believers about their life in Christ, he said, "For you were once in darkness, but now you are light in the Lord. Live as children of light (for the fruit of light consists in all goodness, righteousness and truth)" (Eph. 5:8–9). To the Thessalonian believers he wrote, "We constantly pray for you, that our God may count you worthy of his calling, and that by his power he may fulfill every good purpose of yours and every act prompted by your faith. We pray this so that the name of our Lord Jesus may be glorified in you, and you in him" (2 Thess. 1:11–12).

Goodness is not just what you say but what you do. Those who possess this quality are generous by nature. We can choose to act in good ways as the Holy Spirit continually prompts us to treat people as Jesus would.

ARE PEOPLE BORN GOOD?

Psychology textbooks and self-help books often give the impression that people are born good. Many psychologists maintain the humanistic perspective that if parents provide a loving environment, goodness will naturally come out of a child's life. On the other hand, bad experiences in a child's life are responsible for bad behavior.

Although good or bad experiences can *influence* good or bad behavior, the Bible teaches that each person ultimately chooses his or her behavior. The Scripture is also clear that people aren't born good. Each of us is born with a sinful nature and has an innate tendency to do wrong. We are born in sin, having inherited a disobedient nature from Adam. David said, "Surely I was sinful at birth, sinful from the time my mother conceived me" (Ps. 51:5). Thus we can see that the tendency to do wrong, or sin, is within every human being. Paul informs us that "all have sinned and fall short of the glory of God" (Rom. 3:23). Even without bad childhood relationships and experiences, people are naturally inclined toward sin, rebellion, disobedience, selfishness, exploitation, and greed.

Concerning children and their natural inclination to the sinful nature, founder of Focus on the Family, Dr. James Dobson, said,

They don't have to be taught these behaviors. They are natural expressions of their humanness. Although this perspective is viewed with disdain by the secular world today, the evidence to support it is overwhelming. How else do we explain the pugnacious and perverse nature of every society on earth? Bloody warfare has been the centerpiece of world history for more than 5,000 years. People of every race and creed around the globe have tried to rape, plunder, burn, blast and kill each other century after century. Peace has been but a momentary pause when they stopped to reload! Plato said more than 2,350 years ago, "Only dead men have seen an end to war."

We also find a depressing incidence of murder, drug abuse, child molestation, prostitution, adultery, homosexuality and dishonesty among people. How would we account for this pervasive evil in a world of people who are naturally inclined toward good? Have they really drifted into these anti-social and immoral behaviors despite their inborn tendencies? If so, surely one society in all the world would have been able to preserve the goodness with which children are born. Where is it? Does such a place exist? No, although admittedly some societies are more moral than others. Still, none reflect the harmony that might be expected from the natural-goodness theorists. Why not? Because their basic premise is wrong.[5]

THE SOLUTION

The beginning of a *good* nature starts when we become born again. This means just what it says: we are spiritually *born again* when we surrender our lives to Christ. God does not save us because we are good but because of his incredible mercy, kindness, and goodness. "While we were still sinners, Christ died for us" (Rom. 5:8).

When we become Christians our basic nature changes.

- Before we are Christians we cannot have fellowship with God, because God is holy, pure, and righteous. When we become believers we are reconciled to God (2 Cor. 5:16–21).
- Before we are Christians we can't possibly live a life that is free of sin. When we are born again we become justified (Rom. 3:26).
- Before we are believers we are bound to sin; it is our master. As believers we are set free from sin and are no longer slaves to unrighteousness (Rom. 6:18).
- Before coming to Christ it is impossible to do enough to clear our sinful past, present, and future. When we surrender our lives to Christ and ask for his forgiveness he completely forgives us of all our sins (1 John 1:9).
- Before we are believers, our nature is sinful. After salvation we are new creations in Christ—"the old is gone the new has come!" (2 Cor. 5:17).
- People are created in the image of God; after salvation, however, Christ dwells in us and the Holy Spirit becomes part of our lives (Rom. 8:9; Col. 1:27). Because of that, he will help us to do good. "For it is God who works in you to will and to act according to his good purpose" (Phil. 2:13).
- After we become born-again Christians we are sanctified (Gk. *hagiasmos*), which means to make holy, to consecrate, to separate from the world and be set apart from sin so that we may have an intimate relationship with God. Our sanctification is an immediate act in which we are by God's grace set free from Satan's bondage and are no longer bound to sin (Rom. 6:18; 2 Cor. 5:17; Eph. 2:4–6; Col. 3:1–3), yet it is a progressive act as well. Sanctification is a lifelong process of putting to death sinful activities, feelings, and thinking (Rom. 8:1–17). We are progressively transformed into the image of Christ (2 Cor. 3:18). We grow in God's grace (2 Peter

3:18), and we demonstrate greater love—and the other fruit of the Spirit—toward people (Matt. 22:37–39; 1 John 4:7–8, 11, 20–21).

Goodness is a gift of God. Christians are not sinless; as long as we remain in our earthly bodies we will continue to fall short of perfection. Therefore, we need to die to our sinful natures and walk in the Spirit daily. The difference in our lives before and after being born again is this: before we were Christians our sinful nature had control over us, but now that we are "in Christ" the Holy Spirit helps us control the sinful nature. This is a powerful truth for all of us to understand. You can control your smoking or drinking habit, drug addiction, temper, sexual sin, or whatever problem you may have. When Christ lives in you and you walk with him and give him mastery over your life, you will be free of such debilitating behaviors.

The psalmist David wrote, "Surely goodness and love will follow me all the days of my life" (Ps. 23:6). God's goodness is readily available to all of us, but we must be disciplined and keep our focus on him and on who we are in Christ. Following are several suggestions for learning to live the *good* life.

THE BIBLE IS GOD'S MANUAL ON LIVING A GOOD LIFE

David said, "How CAN a young man keep his way pure? By living according to your word. . . . I have hidden your word in my heart that I might not sin against you" (Ps. 119:9,11). The Bible is God's instruction book that will tell us how to please him, how to treat people, how to have an abundant life, how to avoid sin, and so much more. Paul said that "all Scripture is God-breathed and is useful for teaching, rebuking, correcting and training in righteousness, so that the man of God may be thoroughly equipped for every good work" (2 Tim. 3:16).

Each year the Bible continues to be a best-seller. Most American homes have at least one Bible. It may sit on a coffee table, on a fireplace mantel, or be part of a collection on a bookshelf. Many people read a Bible periodically or talk about what they think the Bible says. God, however, requires that we do more than read the Bible; we are also to do what it says to do. James 1:22 says, "Do not merely listen to the word, and so deceive yourselves. Do what it says." God's Word teaches right behavior and will help us have a good life.

You probably read your mail and possibly a newspaper every day. Maybe you are careful to look at the leading editorials, the latest mutual fund numbers, the sports scores, or something else that is important to you. The Bible is more important than anything else you could read, and it is critical that you know its Author. Like David, we should hide God's Word—grasp and remember its instructions—in our hearts, because, as evangelist D. L. Moody, said, "The Bible will keep you from sin, or sin will keep you from the Bible."[6]

We all experience times when we simply do not know what to do. We want to do the right thing, but we are stuck in a gray area of not knowing what that might be. The Bible not only has specific instructions about what we should or should not do, but it gives us principles about behavior too. Henry Ward Beecher said, "The Bible is God's chart for you to steer by, to keep you from the bottom of the sea, and to show you where the harbor is, and how to reach it without running on rocks or bars."[7]

Many people live their lives with a philosophy of trial and error. They experiment with certain behaviors and beliefs as they try to determine their personal lifestyle or opinions. This is a dangerous way to live. It reminds me of a tragic story that the *New*

York Times wrote on the death of Sam Sebastiani Jr., who was part of one of California's most prominent wine-making families. Mr. Sebastiani died when he ate some poisonous mushrooms he found near his home in Santa Rosa.

> The mushroom Mr. Sebastiani is thought to have eaten was an *Amanita phalloides*, also known as the death-cap mushroom. It is the cause of 95 percent of lethal mushroom poisoning world-wide and is fatal more than 35 percent of the time; toxins in its cap destroy the victim's liver by rupturing the cells.
>
> Experts . . . are warning inexperienced mushroom enthu-siasts to leave the picking to trained mycologists, who will not be fooled by poisonous varieties that closely resemble their non-poisonous cousins.
>
> Roseanne Soloway, a poison-control-center administra-tor, says, "A level of presumed expertise is not enough to save your life."
>
> One of the most sinister aspects of deadly mushroom poi-soning, is the delay between ingestion and onset of symptoms. The stronger the poison, the longer it takes to show itself, and by the time a patient is aware of the problem, it may be too late.[8]

Many people seem to live by their hunches. We do not need to guess, for God has given us his instruction manual. God never intended us to journey through life without instructions about how to live, what to avoid, what to recognize as sin, what behaviors can injure us, and how we can be pleasing to him. Life is full of land mines, and we can learn how to avoid them by reading his book. We do not need to experiment to determine what behavior is right or wrong. We need look no further than the Bible to understand how to have a relationship with God and how to have eternal life.

God's book has all the answers, and we should do everything we can to make it part of our lives.

YOU CAN PROTECT YOURSELF
FROM BAD THOUGHTS

Jesus said, "The eye is the lamp of the body. If your eyes are good, your whole body will be full of light. But if your eyes are bad, your whole body will be full of darkness" (Matt. 6:22), What we choose to look at, read, listen to, and think about will effect how we live. If we are filling our minds with negative, impure, or wrong information, we will struggle in these areas of our life. It is no wonder that our country seems to be becoming more and more violent. One needs only to look at television programming for a few evenings to see how packed full of fighting and killing it is. The morals of our society are in a downward spiral, and as one views today's Hollywood entertainment, it becomes obvious that morals do not guide the producer's script.

Christians are part of the problem. We cannot permit filthy, immoral, spiritually degrading television, videos, or movies to come into our lives without moral consequences. Dr. D. James Kennedy writes in his book *The Gates of Hell Shall Not Prevail,*

> Christians are watching (and thus supporting) many of the objectionable programs on TV. Without doing prior research (for instance, by getting *Movieguide*), Christians are buying tickets for many of the films that denigrate Christianity. Believe it or not, Christian teens are reportedly watching just about as many of the R-rated films as non-Christian teens, according to Dr. Ted Baehr, president of The Christian Film and Television Commission. A recent poll by George Barna shows

that "Christian young adults are more likely than others to have watched *MTV* in the past week"! For example, Barna found that 42 percent of Christian "baby busters" (the generation that followed the "baby boomers") watch *MTV* versus only 33 percent of non-Christian baby busters. That's not good! Clearly we're not going to be part of the solution if we're part of the problem.

What we feed on spiritually—what we put into our souls—will determine our spiritual growth.[9]

We need to wake up to the moral compromise that television programmers consistently offer. Twenty-five homosexual characters were regularly featured on prime-time dramas and sitcoms during the 1998–99 season, according to the Gay and Lesbian Alliance Against Defamation, which lobbied the TV stations and urged them not to run an ad that a coalition of eighteen conservative groups wanted to run in Washington, D.C. The "ex-gay" TV ad that was to be kicked off nationwide had a Mother's Day theme. It showed an elderly mother seated with her son. "My son Michael found out the truth—he could walk away from homosexuality," she says. "But he found out too late. He has AIDS. If you love your children, love them enough to let them know the truth. There is hope for change, hope for the future."

"A decade ago, I walked away from homosexuality through the power of Jesus Christ," says the son as a phone number is displayed. "It's not about hate; it's about hope."[10]

Programmers do not want solid moral truth to come across the airways. They really believe ratings will go up (and they are probably right) when they show sexual innuendoes, blatant moral compromise, violence, and antibiblical themes. They especially do not want commercials or programs that threaten their ungodly lifestyle. While we know this, we still choose to watch and listen.

Think about it. The average American viewer watches an equivalent of fifty-two days of TV a year. By age sixty-five, the average adult will have spent nearly nine years of his or her life watching TV. Every year the average teen spends 900 hours in school and 1,500 hours watching TV. Every week the average child between ages two and eleven watches 1,197 minutes of TV and spends 39 minutes talking with his or her parents. Sixty-six percent of Americans watch TV while eating dinner. Fifty-two percent of kids between ages five and seventeen have a TV set in their bedrooms.[11] There is no question that what we watch and listen to has a tremendous influence on how we think and act. What are you permitting to come into your life?

I (Wayde) have been in the Philippines during the rainy season when the streets sometimes become flooded and the sewage canals are clogged for days. People try to get around in knee-deep (or worse) water, and during these times there is great danger of disease spreading.

In September 1996 Manila was experiencing such a deluge. Uli Schmetzer of the *Chicago Tribune* wrote that three hundred people were suffering from cholera and seven had already died. Flies and cockroaches were feeding on the trash that floated on the surface of the water, and they were the carriers of the cholera germs.

Schmetzer explained that Alfedo Lim, the mayor of Manila, had a unique idea. He offered cash bounty for anyone who brought dead or alive flies or cockroaches to a health official. The reward was 1 peso (4 cents) for every ten flies and 1.5 pesos (6 cents) for every ten cockroaches. The health department highly publicized the program in the poorest areas of Manila. Residents were paid on the spot. The chief of the health department said, "If we kill the flies at once, we can stop the spread of these diseases."[12]

Sinful thoughts are like a deadly disease. Unless we deal with them quickly, they will spread and bring spiritual injury—or even death—on us. James said, "Each one is tempted when, by his own evil desire, he is dragged away and enticed. Then, after desire has conceived, it gives birth to sin; and sin, when it is full-grown, gives birth to death" (James 1:14–15). When we are tempted to look at, read, or talk about something that is sinful, we need turn from it at once rather than dwelling on it and allowing it to spawn negative behavior. The more we prevent the spread of sinful thoughts, the less we will have to wrestle with them.

Our mind is a precious commodity, and we need to do all we can to protect it. We cannot just fill it with wrong thinking or impure or violent images and expect that we will simply be able to turn off such thoughts and images when they begin to come into focus. We must guard our mind, and the Bible tells us how. Paul said, "Whatever is true, whatever is noble, whatever is right, whatever is pure, whatever is lovely, whatever is admirable—if anything is excellent or praiseworthy—think about such things" (Phil. 4:8). We make a conscious decision to think about what we should be thinking about. We make a decision to reject harmful thoughts and think about good things. God will help.

Throughout life you will be faced with decisions about what is right or wrong, good or bad, ethical or unethical. Developing sensitivity to your conscience is critical, and it takes courage to take a stand on your own. For some this may seem impossible or at least very frightening, because there is a perception that we need to go along with the crowd in order to be part of the crowd. This kind of thinking has gotten a lot of people into trouble.

On the other hand, it is good to be around people who are full of God's wisdom and go to church and those in our schools or career fields who are good at what they do. Good qualities rub off on us too.

The book of Daniel tells the fascinating story of four young men who determined to be loyal to God no matter what the cost.

Daniel, Hananiah, Mishael, and Azariah were among those who were taken from Jerusalem to Babylonia when Babylon besieged the city. These young men were selected to be trained for the king's service. For three years they were to be trained and educated and taught the language and literature of the Babylonians. Certain foods were to be included in their diet, but Daniel felt that he should not partake of them. "Daniel resolved not to defile himself with the royal food and wine" (Dan. 1:8). When he asked permission to eat the food his religion permitted, the supervisor approved for his friends and him to do it for ten days, then he would observe how they were doing. To his surprise, "at the end of the ten days they looked healthier and better nourished than any of the young men who ate the royal food" (v. 15).

Later King Nebuchadnezzar made a huge gold image of himself and ordered the people to fall down and worship the image. Again the young Jewish men were conscientious objectors. They simply could not do it. Their God was the only being they would ever worship. When the crowd fell down to worship the image, the loyal companions of Daniel didn't budge. This infuriated the king, and he threatened them that if they did not obey they would be thrown into a blazing furnace. Their response? "O Nebuchadnezzar, we do not need to defend ourselves before you in this matter. If we are thrown into the blazing furnace, the God we serve is able to save us from it, and he will rescue us from your hand, O king. But even if he does not; we want you to know, O king, that we will not serve your gods or worship the image of gold you have set up" (Dan. 3:16–18). The king did throw the three young men into the furnace, but God met them there. When the king looked into the furnace, he said, "Look! I see four men walking around in the fire, unbound and unharmed, and the fourth looks like a son of the gods" (v. 25).

Later Daniel was commanded not to pray to anyone but the

king. You can guess Daniel's response. He didn't stop praying to his God for even a day. Again his decision to be obedient to God got him into trouble. He was put into a den of lions to be killed. The lions, however, were not interested in eating Daniel. The next day, when being removed from the den, Daniel said, "O king, live forever! My God sent his angel, and he shut the mouths of the lions. They have not hurt me, because I was found innocent in his sight" (Dan. 6:21–22).

Over and over we see in the lives of Daniel and his friends the commitment to be obedient to their godly convictions and to be different from the crowd. Before they were taken into captivity, before the Scripture said, "Daniel resolved not to defile himself" (1:8), before they were faced with decisions about what was right or wrong, they made a decision in their hearts to serve the Lord no matter what. Even if they lost friends, reputation, or rewards or endangered their lives, they would not compromise.

Peter reminds us, "Who is going to harm you if you are eager to do good? But even if you should suffer for what is right, you are blessed" (1 Peter 3:13–14). Doing good is a commitment to make right decisions in matters of conscience and in our motivations for helping people. We do good even when we are not recognized. We have no ulterior motives for our good treatment of others; we do it because God wants us to treat people well. Our hearts should be so full of the goodness of God that it becomes a natural way of treating people and the thought of any kind of reward doesn't cross our minds.

God naturally shows us goodness, and this same fruit comes from our lives because he dwells in us. Paul complimented the Roman Christians by saying they were "full of goodness" (Rom. 15:14). Rome was very probably the city where Paul was imprisoned and consequently martyred for his faith, yet he found a group of believers that did not "do as the Romans" did, and he became a recipient of their goodness. They found a way to give to him when he could do nothing in return.

It is a little frightening to decide to be different. You may think, "If I treat people this way, they will take advantage of me or use me." Or you may think this kind of behavior is weak or without courage. This simply isn't the case. It takes a lot more strength to swim against the current than to float with it. People will respect you for your decision not to go with the crowd.

THE HOLY SPIRIT WILL SPEAK TO YOU THROUGH YOUR CONVICTIONS

A popular twenty-first-century theory is that we need to be "open minded" and willing to accept new ideas, philosophies, religious beliefs, and lifestyles. This has given new focus to the old thought that there is more than one road to heaven. These supposedly open-minded people would say, "All religions really have the same goal in mind, and God understands that." Many have a problem with a literal hell because they can't imagine God sending anyone to such a horrible place. Perhaps you have heard of some denominational groups that are considering approval of homosexual marriages, partly because they have determined that some people are created to be homosexuals. Or perhaps you have read or heard that a denomination has decided that the Bible has some errors in it. Among their reasons for this conclusion is that they have a difficult time believing that the miracles recorded in the Bible are literal.

One of the greatest challenges for the church of the future new millennium is whether it will be a church of conviction. There will be more sophisticated ways to sin, such as technological advances that open the door for secret sin, and outright, bold challenges to the Christian faith. The only thing that will keep you safe from this onslaught of the enemy is your commitment to obey your godly convictions.

One example of an escalating problem is increased Internet usage. While this is a tremendous tool for research, communication, and business, it also has a negative side. Pornography (at every level) is being introduced to children, teens, and adults who quickly become addicted to this hideous sin. Because of their ability to purchase Web sites, use chat rooms, talk to strangers, and do creative promotional activities, the people who are involved in the business of pornography have discovered a gold mine.[13] Millions of people are now involved with pornography. As a result, lives, marriages, and futures are being greatly injured, even destroyed.

A new *CNN/Time* poll of teens between the ages of thirteen and seventeen reveals that 82 percent have used the Internet. Of these online kids, 44 percent have viewed sites with "information on sex" and 25 percent have seen "hate group" sites. Forty-five percent believe that their parents know only "a little" about their Web activities, while 43 percent say their parents have no rules governing how much time they can spend online or what sites they are allowed to visit. Another 26 percent say their parents have set rules, but they don't always follow them.[14]

What will protect you from pornographic sites on the Internet? Your decision to obey godly convictions. What will protect you from negative, time-wasting television programming? Your decision to obey godly convictions. What will keep you from renting an X-or even R-rated video? Your decision to obey your godly convictions. What will keep you from walking into a theater that is showing a film that is full of compromise and sinful actions? Again, your decision to obey your godly convictions.

Our struggle to guard ourselves from sin is not going to get any easier. Technology will continue to advance and will bring with it opportunities to become involved in either good or bad behavior. Getting involved in sinful activities will be increasingly easy to do in the privacy of your home, when no one is looking. But God will always be near and will help you decide what is right or wrong. He will give you convictions that you can choose to obey.

Paul said, "Hate what is evil; cling to what is good" (Rom. 12:9). There is no question that we are to know what is evil and what is good and make a conscious decision to avoid the one and get close to the other.

Our generation reminds me of the warning Isaiah gave: "Woe to those who call evil good and good evil, who put darkness for light and light for darkness" (Isa. 5:20). Many in our day call good behaviors, good thinking, and good plans evil. Many call evil behaviors, evil thinking, and evil plans good. Following are some examples of this confused thinking.

- Our generation teaches that before birth a being in its mother's womb is only a fetus, therefore, because it is not a person, it can be destroyed if the mother desires. Because of this opinion, over a million babies are murdered in America every year. We have celebrities, like Roseanne, who say; "You know who else I can't stand is them [sic] people that are anti-abortion. [Expletive deleted] them, I hate them. . . . They're horrible, they're hideous people. They're ugly, old, geeky, hideous men. . . . They just don't want nobody [sic] to have an abortion 'cause they want you to keep spitting out kids so they can [expletive deleted] molest them."[15]
- Our generation teaches that we need to give children condoms because they can't control their sexual appetite.
- Our generation teaches that homosexuality is a created physical nature just as heterosexuality is.

- Our generation challenges the inerrancy of the Bible.
- Our generation disputes the miracles found in the Bible and says they were only stories used to make a point.
- Our generation teaches that prayer in school should not be permitted.
- Our generation removes manger scenes from school lawns while permitting witches to be accepted into the military chaplaincy.
- Our generation creates technology that can be useful in elementary, junior high, and high school classrooms, school libraries, and public libraries, yet it provides access through this technology to photographs, written materials, and advertising that is clearly destructive—all in the name of freedom.

Why does God want us to cling to what is good and hate what is evil? Because he loves us and wants us to have an abundant life. He also wants us to influence this evil world for good. Because the Holy Spirit dwells in every believer, he will help us be sensitive to what is good so that we can avoid what is evil. When we read the Bible we begin to understand what behaviors are best for us, how God thinks, and how we should live. When we pray God will speak to us about our convictions (what we are to believe and what we are to disbelieve). When we have a conviction, like Daniel and his friends, we must resolve to stand by it. This takes great courage.

Both Wayde and I remember when we first decided to live for God and walk away from the ways of the world. Our friends who were compromising or living in ways that were obviously sinful didn't want us to leave their way of living. They even tried to persuade us to "get back in" and reject our new commitment to serve the Lord. When we decided that we would never return to our old ways, we lost their friendship. That was okay, because our decision to follow our Christian convictions held a tremendous reward. It gave us a peace and assurance that this world could never provide. You may not be popular when you decide to obey your godly convictions, but as Peter says, if you "suffer for doing good and you endure it, this is commendable before God" (1 Peter 2:20). Not everyone will agree with you, but you will have been obedient, and you will make a difference in a world that calls good evil and evil good.

If you are going to develop goodness in your life, you must also grow in your courage to be different from your generation. Life can harden us and make us insensitive to people. We can develop a survival attitude of doing whatever needs to be done to make it in life, let alone get ahead. But God wants us to have tender, trusting hearts—hearts that sincerely desire to be good to people even when they will take advantage of us.

COURAGE TO DO GOOD, COURAGE TO GIVE YOUR ALL

The echoes of Littleton, Colorado, will be heard for years to come. At Columbine High School in the spring of 1999 fifteen people lost their lives. Among those are incredible stories of courage.

Mark Taylor was wounded while sharing his faith in Christ with two Mormon students.

Eyewitnesses said Rachel Scott received four gunshot wounds. Just before the fatal shot, the gunman asked if she believed in God. Rachel answered yes, and the gunman said, "Then go be with Him."[16]

Lori Johnson, a leader in Rachel's youth group, said, "She had two dreams: she wanted to make an impact for God, and she wanted to live in His presence all the time. It's amazing to me that God has fulfilled both."[17]

CNN televised Rachel's funeral to millions as an estimated three thousand people gathered at Trinity Christian Center. On her casket dozens of statements were written:

- "I'm proud that you stood up for Christ, and I'll see you in heaven."
- Rachel's mother wrote, "Honey, you are everything a mother could ask the Lord for in a daughter: I love you so much."
- "Rachel, I love you so very much. I will always miss you. You are such a strong person. To know you're in a better place. Your memory will always live in me. I will miss you forever."
- "Rachel, you are my hero and I love you with all of my heart. You're in a better place with Jesus now. Again I love you."
- "Rachel, you were very brave. You were loved by all."

We who are parents can't imagine the incredible pain involved in the loss of a child. But Rachel's mother, Beth Nimmo, boldly proclaimed, "The enemy bit off more than he could chew by attacking the Christian element in Columbine. He's going to pay far more than he thought he'd pay by taking these kids. He's going to be sorry because it's producing a whole generation who are taking a stand for the gospel."[18]

Another student said the gunmen asked her if she believed in God, and she said, "Yes I do. That's what my parents taught me." They shot her six times, but she lived.

John Tomlin, sixteen, had plans to return to Mexico after helping the poor in the summer of 1998. John was killed in the library.

Among the martyrs was Cassie Bernall, who, when looking down the barrel of a gun and into the eyes of a killer, was asked if she believed in God. Without hesitation Cassie said, "Yes." With

THE FRUIT OF THE SPIRIT

that last statement she was shot and killed. Cassie's faith was the most important thing in her life. Even when faced with the knowledge that she could be shot, she didn't budge.

Cassie's mother and father said, "Our prayer is that her yes will be proclaimed aloud by many more to come."[19]

Val Schnurr, eighteen, affirmed her faith in God after watching Cassie die. And certainly there are many others who have decided to make a stand for Christ, for goodness, because they watched these teenagers live and die with such courage. Schnurr survived nine bullets and shrapnel wounds.

~

Goodness. It flows from our good God, who is full of mercy, kindness, and love. Goodness is something we decide to do because we belong to him. In a world full of pain, heartache, and hatred we are asked to be good and to demonstrate God's love. Although this may be difficult, it will show those around you that the gospel really does make a difference in a person's life.

CHAPTER 7

FAITHFULNESS

The Foundation of True Friendship

For millennia the North Star has shined brilliantly, giving direction to land travelers, sailors, and pilots. When south seems to look like north, and east seems to look like west, many look for the North Star because they know they can trust it.

People also have always enjoyed watching shooting stars. These bright stars seem to come out of nowhere. As quickly as they catch our attention they fade and burn out. Though they are beautiful, they are not a dependable compass like the North Star.

The fruit of faithfulness is trustworthiness and steadfastness of character in the life of a believer. The Greek word for this fruit, *pistis*, is translated, among other things, as "faith," "belief," and "trusted." Those who are faithful are dependable, and we can place our trust in them.

God is our best example of faithfulness; he will never break his promises to you. Paul reminded his friend Timothy that even "if we are faithless, [God] will remain faithful" (2 Tim. 2:13), for it is his very nature. You can absolutely trust him and his Word. Not doing what he said he would do is out of the realm of possibility. God wants us to be faithful like him, and as with the producing of all fruit, this is possible only as we stay connected to Jesus, the Vine.

The Scriptures are also full of stories of people who were faithful to God. Hebrews 11, for example, tells of many Old Testament people who demonstrated unprecedented loyalty to God.

We are to be faithful in our relationships with our spouses, children, parents, employers, employees, friends, and people in general. Most of all, we are to be faithful in our obedience to the Lord. One day when we meet him face-to-face we will not be judged on our success, our educational achievements, or even on all that we may have given. We will be judged on how faithful we were to all that God asked us to do. You and I want to hear the beautiful words, "Well done, good and faithful servant!" (Matt. 25:23).

BEING FRIENDS WITH GOD

Abraham was called God's friend (Isa. 41:8). What an amazing thought! We all know—or should know—that God loves us. He desires a relationship with us, and in fact, believers are called his children (John 1:12–13). But being God's friend is a different kind of relationship, unique in its level of trust and respect. Friendship involves openness in communication, vulnerability, transparency, and a sharing of ideas, dreams, and goals. Friendship is special and is to be cherished.

Why was Abraham called God's friend? "Abraham believed God" (James 2:23), and God could count on him to be faithful in all that he asked him to do. The fascinating story of Abraham gives us example after example of a man who simply trusted God at his word and was passionate about being obedient even when he didn't understand.

Jesus called his disciples his friends. He said, "I no longer call you servants, because a servant does not know his master's business. Instead, I have called you friends, for everything that I learned from my Father I have made known to you" (John 15:15). Friends share information and communicate on a deeper level. They trust that if something shared needs to be kept confidential, it will be. Friendship involves dependence, relationship, respect, and confidentiality.

Jesus also said to his disciples "You are my friends if you do what I command" (John 15:14). Why did he add a requirement? I believe it has to do with trust. Jesus knows what is best for us. He knows what will work in our lives and what will injure us. Doing his will is doing what will help us in the long and the short run. When people don't obey God's principles they not only show that they want to "do their own thing," they also show that they do not trust God. They wonder if God is right or if he will come through for them. With friendship comes trust, the assurance that the friend will keep his or her word.

You may wonder, How can I be called a friend of Jesus? I still wrestle with temptation and sin and am by no means perfect. Why would he want to be friends with me? Those of us who love Christ desire to do better and be more like him. We all have to deal daily with temptation and strive to be more Christlike in our actions, thinking, and feelings. He understands our motives. He sees potential in us that many of us would not believe, and he sees promise in the worst of sinners. We should too.

Philip Yancey writes in his book *The Jesus I Never Knew*,

> When Jesus came to earth, demons recognized him, the sick
> flocked to him, and sinners doused his feet and head with

perfume. Meanwhile he offended pious Jews with their strict preconceptions of what God should be like. Their rejection makes me wonder, *Could religious types be doing just the reverse now? Could we be perpetuating an image of Jesus that fits our pious expectations but does not match the person portrayed so vividly in the Gospels?*

Jesus was the friend of sinners. He commended a groveling tax collector over a God-fearing Pharisee. The first person to whom he openly revealed himself as Messiah was a Samaritan woman who had a history of five failed marriages and was currently living with yet another man. With his dying breath he pardoned a thief who would have zero opportunity for spiritual growth. . . . I view with amazement Jesus' uncompromising blend of graciousness toward sinners and hostility toward sin, because in much of church history I see virtually the opposite. We give lip service to "hate the sin while loving the sinner," but how well do we practice this principle?[1]

We Christians are all sinners who have been saved by grace. Some of us have stories that we aren't anxious to tell, but before we came to Christ, Jesus saw something in us. He decided to take a risk on us and attempt friendship even though we were not living for him and could reject his love. He chooses to remain our Friend even though we are not perfect. He understands our struggles and continually prays for us and stays loyal to us.

The idea of being a friend of God is puzzling to many believers. But if you have given your life to Christ, that is what you are. Are you trying to develop this friendship? Do you want to be with Jesus? Do you talk often to him? Do you communicate your deepest concerns, worries, and struggles to him? Do you want to be with him? Do you want to be more like him? Do you trust him?

Like Abraham, we are friends of God. Our faith is to be like

Abraham's. He was obedient to God and trusted him. We too must be obedient to God and trust him in all we do.

FAITHFULNESS IS A SIGN OF MATURITY

One of the main qualities I look for when choosing a person to run a program or lead a department is whether candidates are faithful to do what they say they will do. This may be demonstrated in their completing assigned tasks in the time period we have discussed, or, if there is an unforeseen obstacle, speaking to me about it so it can be resolved in a timely manner. I notice if they are disciplined with their time, if they keep their word, if they complete the job, and, in the process, if they treat people well. Does it seem that being responsible is critical to them, or do they just do the job because they are interested in the financial remuneration? One major sign of immaturity is a person's refusal to accept responsibility.

Our children may want money and the privileges of being an adult, but if they cannot handle money correctly or get up in time for school, college, or their job, they have not learned responsibility, and it is not wise to give them privileges. A lot of people want to be supervisors, managers, and leaders, but any employer who puts people in charge who don't understand responsibility will injure the organization.

God's kingdom is organized in such a way that if we are faithful in the small things, we will be given more responsibility (see Matt. 25:21, 23). Spending time reading and studying the Bible, being consistent in our prayer lives, and obeying God's will are all part of maturity in Christ. God has given all of us certain responsibilities. When we disobey or refuse to accept what God has asked us to do, we are unfaithful. But doing all that God has asked us to do is a sign of spiritual maturity.

You may say, "I have a long way to go in this area of faithfulness." Perhaps you feel frustrated by your failure to follow through on some commitments you have made. One of the greatest truths you can understand is that you can improve. You will become more faithful to God and godly commitments as you are transformed into Christ's likeness. Paul wrote to the Galatian believers, "I am again in the pains of childbirth until Christ is formed in you" (Gal. 4:19). The word "formed" (Gk. *morphō*) means "the inward and real formation of the essential nature of a person." Paul would agonize until Christ was formed in these believers. His concern was that they would demonstrate the character, or fruit, of Christ. This Greek term was used to describe the formation and development of an embryo in a mother's womb. Paul wrote in Romans 12:2, "Do not conform any longer to the pattern of this world, but be transformed" (Gk. *metamorphō*). This word is the root word for the English word *metamorphosis*. A caterpillar is formed and developed (transformed) into a beautiful butterfly. As we grow in the grace of God we are transformed and we become more faithful, loving, and gentle. The fruit is more evident in our lives after years of walking with Christ than in the beginning when we first become Christians.

If you are concerned that you are not faithful enough or do not have enough joy or that you do not love people with the depth that you feel the Lord wants you to, understand that when you walk in God's Spirit you are being transformed and that as you grow you will develop. But you must hunger to grow in his fruit and determine to permit God to form Christ in you.

Dr. Lewis Sperry Chafer, the founder of Dallas Theological Seminary, was a creative, visionary, and unique individual. On one occasion he was asked to speak at a banquet. The audience had sat through three hours of preliminaries, such as announcements, music, presentations, and acknowledgments. Sensitive to the time, Dr. Chafer stepped to the podium and began,

> My subject is the Reasonableness of Fully Surrendering Our Lives to God. Reason number one: He is all-wise and knows better than anyone else what is best for my life. Reason number two: He is almighty and has the power to accomplish that which is best for me. Reason number three: He loves me more than anyone else in the world loves me. Conclusion: Therefore the most logical thing the Christian can do is to surrender his life completely to God. What more can I say? What more need I say?[2]

That was his message, and what a powerful message it was. He could have talked for hours—and put everyone to sleep—but the truth rests in the simple fact that "the most logical thing the Christian can do is surrender his life completely to God." When we do so, fruit, such as faithfulness, will naturally become apparent in our lives.

THE STORY OF FAITHFULNESS

In the parable of the talents (Matt. 25:14–30), Jesus gave us two examples of people who were faithful and one who was not. The two who were faithful took what their master gave them and invested it wisely. The third man either was afraid of his master ("you are a hard man," v. 24) or was lazy and didn't take advantage of the opportunity that was given him. Possibly he was both.

We can learn at least four truths from this parable: God gives everyone different gifts, more responsibility is good, people who

THE FRUIT OF THE SPIRIT

are lazy with God's talents are punished, and only people who invest get a return.

God Gives Everyone Different Gifts

"To one he gave five talents of money, to another two talents, and to another one talent, each according to his ability" (Matt. 25:15). Some people have many talents and are capable of multiple responsibilities. In the parable the master determined the amount of talents each servant was capable of handling well. The master was only concerned about how each man used the talents he was given.

Some have the idea that God will give greater rewards to those who have incredible gifts and abilities. This is a wrong assumption. God rewards us according to how we *use* our gifts. He is watching our stewardship as we develop and invest our gifts. God will never say, "I wish you had had that gift and used it for my kingdom." He doesn't compare us to anyone else. He will reward us according to how we used what *we* had. We do not have the same talents, abilities, or gifts as others; however, we do possess the same ability to be faithful with what we have.

More Responsibility Is Good

"Well done, good and faithful servant! You have been faithful with a few things; I will put you in charge of many things" (Matt. 25:21, 23).

The two servants who invested their talents well received more responsibility, yet all responsibility was removed from the one who did nothing with his talent. In God's kingdom responsibility is given to those who can handle it. Will your attitude be humble; will you work hard with what you have and remain loyal in the process? If something needs to be done and no one else will do it, will you be willing to step up to the plate and swing? If so, God will help you in your effort to do good. You will be able to look back with gratefulness that you stepped out by faith.

In his book *When God Whispers Your Name*, Max Lucado tells the story of a man named John Egglen who had never preached a sermon in his life:

> Wasn't that he didn't want to, just never needed to. But then one morning he did. The snow left his town of Colchester, England, buried in white. When he awoke on that January Sunday in 1850, he thought of staying home. Who would go to church in such weather?
>
> But he reconsidered. He was, after all, a deacon. And if the deacons didn't go, who would? So he put on his boots, hat, and coat and walked the six miles to the Methodist church.
>
> He wasn't the only member who considered staying home. In fact, he was one of the few who came. Only thirteen people were present. Twelve members and one visitor. Even the minister was snowed in. Someone suggested they go home. Egglen would hear none of that. They'd come this far; they would have a service. Besides, they had a visitor. A thirteen-year-old-boy.
>
> But who would preach? Egglen was the only deacon. It fell to him.
>
> And so he did. His sermon lasted only three minutes. It drifted and wandered and made no point in an effort to make several. But at the end, an uncharacteristic courage settled upon the man. He lifted his eyes and looked straight at the boy and challenged: "Young man, look to Jesus, Look! Look! Look!"
>
> Did the challenge make a difference? Let the boy, now a man, answer. "I did look, and then and there the cloud on my heart lifted, the darkness rolled away, and at the moment I saw the sun."

The boy's name? Charles Haddon Spurgeon. England's prince of preachers.[3]

Some people do not want more responsibility. In fact, they look forward to getting rid of it. In God's kingdom, however, we are always asked to put forth a 100-percent effort to use the gifts God has given us.

People Who Are Lazy with God's Talents Are Punished

"Take the talent from him and give it to the one who has the ten talents. . . . And throw that worthless servant outside, into the darkness, where there will be weeping and gnashing of teeth" (Matt. 25:28, 30).

The servant who had one talent did nothing with it except bury it, forget about it, and go on with his life. His master called him lazy and wicked. He could have at least deposited it with the bankers and received some interest, but he didn't even have the discipline to do that.

We all know people who work hard and have much to show for their efforts. Not long ago I stayed in the beautiful home of a Romanian immigrant who had moved to the United States with his family just a few years earlier. When they arrived in the United States they had very few material possessions and were poor, but they were determined. Over the years, they have been faithful to God, have worked hard, have invested well, and are givers. They now own more than a hundred rental apartments and use their talent in business to bless God's kingdom. This ability came to them one dollar at a time and one apartment at a time. They were anything but lazy with what God had given them. They did not say, "I have so little, how can I make it in America?" They said, "Look at all the possibilities in this land of opportunity. With God's help we can invest what we have and receive great interest." They worked hard, invested wisely, and have given the glory to God.

Only People Who Invest Get a Return

"For everyone who has will be given more, and he will have an abundance" (Matt. 25:29).

Farmers know that they have to plant their seed by faith, water it, and take care of it. If they do not plant it, they will have only weeds in their fields. "Use it or lose it!" This truth has a parallel in God's kingdom. When by faith we use the talent God has given us, care for it, and work at it, we will get better and be given more. That will never be taken from us. People who practice get better. If, however, we decide not to be faithful with our God-given talents, they will be taken from us.

In 1972 NASA launched an exploratory space probe called *Pioneer 10*. The probe was designed to reach Jupiter, take pictures, and transmit the information back to earth. *Time* reporter Leon Jaroff explained that this bold effort required that the probe not only travel the distance (no probe had ever gone past Mars), but that it also would need to pass through Jupiter's magnetic field, radiation belts, and atmosphere. One of the major concerns was that *Pioneer 10* would be destroyed going through the asteroid belt before it could reach its destination.

As we know, *Pioneer 10* fulfilled its assignment. In fact, when it flew by Jupiter in November 1973, the planet's tremendous gravity pitched the probe with greater speed into the solar system. At 1 billion miles from the sun the tiny probe passed Saturn then flew past Uranus at some 2 billion miles, Neptune at nearly 3 billion miles, and Pluto at almost 4 billion miles. By 1997, twenty-five years after NASA said good-bye to *Pioneer 10*, it was more than 6 billion miles from the sun.

This probe that was designed to be useful for approximately three years continued to signal back to earth from incredible distances far beyond its original assignment.

Jaroff writes, "Perhaps most remarkable, those signals emanate from an 8-watt transmitter, which radiates about as much power as a bedroom night light, and take more than nine hours to reach Earth."[4]

Similar to *Pioneer 10*, you have tremendous potential to be more than you may think is possible. As you remain faithful to what God has given you and continually strive to be obedient to his will, he will stretch you and develop you in many ways. As Chuck Swindoll has said,

> Don't expect wisdom to come into your life like great chunks of rock on a conveyor belt. It isn't like that. It's not splashy and bold . . . nor is it dispensed like a prescription across a counter. Wisdom comes privately from God as a by-product of right decisions, godly reactions, and the application of spiritual principles to daily circumstances. Wisdom comes . . . not from trying to do great things for God . . . but more from being faithful to the small, obscure tasks few people ever see.[5]

What can you do? What has God blessed you with? How are you investing it for God's glory? Are you lazy or are you growing in maturity? Don't waste the talent God has given you.

BEING FAITHFUL TO OUR FRIENDS

Faithfulness is demonstrated in our relationships with people as well as in our relationship with God. Proverbs 17:17 tells us, "A friend loves at all times." Faithfulness is critical to friendship. You may have heard the phrase "fair weather friends," referring to people who like to be around you when everything is going well, when there are no complications, and when you agree on almost everything. When things are a little rough in the relationship, or you disagree, the friend leaves. The friend is only there when things feel right to him or her. True friends, however, are committed and "love" at all times. They understand that disagreements and differences do not have to injure a friendship. In fact, true friends are committed to not forsaking each other (see Prov. 27:10).

Recently, a friend I (Wayde) went to college with called to let me know he had moved to another part of the country. A few years earlier he had lost his very successful job and for the last four years had been trying to rebuild his life and begin another career. For about a year he was without a paying job. Doors were not opening for him to get back into his career field. He couldn't sell his home, so he rented it out and moved to an apartment that was less expensive. The man wasn't lazy, and he sincerely tried to do all he could to make ends meet. In fact, he volunteered to help at a church (forty to fifty hours a week) in his free time.

During that year, I called him or he called me weekly. We talked; I tried to encourage him, and we prayed together. One day early in that first year I thought, *I'm going to call ten to twenty people who know this person and ask them to make a financial commitment to him for one year.* Another friend and I called people and asked if they could assist this person by sending him about $100 monthly. In a few hours we were able to raise over $1000—all from his friends. His life began to move in a more positive direction.

Until he called recently, I had forgotten the situation. He called to say that he was doing great and was experiencing much success in his new job. He also said, "Without your encouragement and help during that first year, I wouldn't have made it."

Ecclesiastes 4:10 says, "If one falls down, his friend can help him up, But pity the man who falls and has no one to help him up!" Genuine friends can be counted on when crisis hits. Practical help in such times is faithfulness with shoes on it.

Are you loyal to your friends? Can your friends count on you to be there? Have you told them that you are committed to telling them the truth, praying for them, and being loyal to them? If not, can you find the time to tell them soon?

KEEPING OUR COMMITMENTS

I am often asked to give recommendations for persons who want jobs, particularly pastoral positions in churches. At times I am hesitant to recommend persons because they have had a history of not fulfilling commitments. They have quit too soon, left their previous position in a wrong way, or left things undone so that it was difficult for the person who followed them. Instead, I must caution the person or church that is interested in the individual. On the other hand, when pastors have been faithful to do their best and have fulfilled their commitments, I am able to give outstanding recommendations.

Dependability, punctuality, and being responsible are all part of the package of faithfulness. Jesus said, "Whoever can be trusted with very little can also be trusted with much, and whoever is dishonest with very little will also be dishonest with much" (Luke 16:10). When your employer, supervisor, or friend counts on you to do something, do you come through?

We face challenges in the work we do that require our faithfulness. For instance, sometimes our work is boring or tedious. I have talked to people who have the kinds of jobs where this issue is a real concern. Perhaps they flip hamburgers for McDonald's. My advice to them is, "Become the best hamburger flipper you can be. Study the art of flipping hamburgers. Ask great burger people how they do it so well, and become an expert in the field." We can find a challenge in everything we do. Most of the time it depends on our attitude.

Another challenge is the amount of work we are asked to do. At times it seems overwhelming. Add to the amount of work the interruptions of phone calls, e-mail, letters, and coworkers. I have met people who simply do not answer their letters or e-mail and do not return their phone calls. My personal policy is to try to return every phone call the day it is received. If I can't, I ask my secretary to let the caller know when I will be able to return his or her call. I answer e-mail in a similar way. If I do not have time to give a complete answer to someone's question, I briefly respond and let the person know that I will answer more fully soon. Then, when I have a window of time, I get back to him or her. Letters need to be answered. When people have taken the time to ask a question, voice a concern, or give a kind word, they deserve a response.

We also need to be trustworthy with the finances of the organization for which we work. Some of us with expense accounts eat at very expensive restaurants and stay at luxurious hotels or spend the maximum allowed. We need to be good stewards and try to live as we would on our own personal budgets. Being sensitive to your employer is part of being faithful. Jesus said, "If you have not been trustworthy with someone else's property, who will give you property of your own?" (Luke 16:12). Your employer has hired you for a particular amount of time each week. Do you show up on time? Do you take too many breaks and long lunches? Do you leave early? What about those for whom you don't directly work but who assume you will be careful with what they own? How do you treat rental cars, hotel room accessories, or something you have borrowed? Are you trustworthy?

Faithfulness is practical in the way it is lived out. It is a lifestyle that people depend on and that God is very aware of when he sees it in our lives. Paul instructed the Colossian believers, "Whatever you do, work at it with all your heart, as working for the Lord, not for men, since you know that you will receive an inheritance from the Lord as a reward. It is the Lord Christ you are serving" (Col. 3:23–24).

Ray Steadman relates an incident in his book *Talking to My Father* that shows the eternal results of faithfulness.

An old missionary couple had been working in Africa for years, and they were returning to New York City to retire. They had no pension; their health was broken; they were booked on the same ship as President Teddy Roosevelt, who was returning from one of his big-game hunting expeditions.

No one paid attention to them. They watched the fanfare that accompanied the President's entourage, with passengers trying to catch a glimpse of the great man.

As the ship moved across the ocean, the old missionary said to his wife, "Something is wrong. Why should we have given our lives in faithful service for God in Africa all these many years and have no one care a thing about us? Here this man comes back from a hunting trip and everybody makes much over him, but nobody gives two hoots about us."

"Dear, you shouldn't feel that way," his wife said.

"I can't help it; it doesn't seem right."

When the ship docked in New York, a band was waiting to greet the President. The mayor and other dignitaries were there. The papers were full of the President's arrival, but no one noticed the missionary couple. They slipped off the ship and found a cheap flat on the East Side, hoping the next day to see what they could do to make a living in the city.

That night the man's spirit broke. He said to his wife, "I can't take this; God is not treating us fairly."

His wife replied, "Why don't you go in the bedroom and tell that to the Lord?"

A short time later he came out from the bedroom, but now his face was completely different. His wife asked, "Dear, what happened?"

"The Lord settled it with me," he said, "I told him how bitter I was that the President should receive this tremendous homecoming, when *no one* met us as we returned home. And when I finished, it seemed as though the Lord put his hand on my shoulder and simply said, *"But you're not home yet!"*[6]

The reward for faithfulness is knowing that you have been obedient and understanding that one day God will say, "Welcome home, my faithful servant! "

CHAPTER 8

GENTLENESS

The Strength of Being Tender

At one time or another all of us have wished that we could take back something we said. Maybe it was an impulsive harsh word or sharp tone of voice we used toward our spouse or children. Perhaps it was rudeness or disrespect toward an employee, neighbor, or someone who took the parking spot we wanted. Or maybe we verbally wiped out someone we felt needed to be put in his or her place. After we got it off our chest, we felt terrible. We had wronged the person and grieved the Holy Spirit, and we had to decide whether we would apologize or stuff our inappropriate behavior deep inside.

Gentleness is a fruit of the Spirit that is fundamental to our relationships, especially those that can keep us on edge—those with people who are pushy or offensive, who live in so much private pain that they reject our attempts to get close, or who have caused us to lose patience either because of our own weariness or their lack of self-control.

In our world of "say what you feel," we are encouraged to give people a mouthful of words that will put them in their place or make our point. If you want to grow in gentleness, television is not a good venue to imitate, for today's programming is full of people screaming at, cussing out, and threatening people in their families or in other relationships. In fact, television may be a major contributor to much of the hostility we see and read about.

Gentleness is a disposition that is even-tempered, tranquil, unpretentious, and has its passions under control. Depending on the context, the New International Version translates the root *praos* into three different English words—"meek" (Matt. 5:5), "humility" (Titus 3:2), and "gentleness" (Gal. 5:23). Gentleness is not to be misunderstood as weakness or a lack of internal strength. In fact, it means quite the opposite: strength under control. People who are mature in this quality pardon and forgive those who have injured them, know when to speak words of correction and when to remain quiet, and rule their own spirits. They understand the strength of being tender.

The Greeks used *praos* when describing a wild animal that had been tamed. Picture a racehorse that has been disciplined to do exactly what its rider instructs it to do. It knows when to run with all of its tremendous strength and when to pace itself as it rounds the track. Christians who have grown in gentleness are balanced— they don't overreact or underreact. They have learned temperance in their personal responsibilities, conversation, and decisions, and they understand when assertiveness or remaining quiet is in order. Gentleness is balanced and disciplined.

Concerning this fruit, Chuck Swindoll writes,

> Immediately, we may get the wrong impression. . . . In our rough
> and rugged individualism, we think of gentleness as weakness,
> being soft, and virtually spineless. Not so! The Greek term is
> extremely colorful, helping us grasp a correct understanding of
> why the Lord sees the need for servants to be gentle.

Carefully chosen words that soothe strong emotions are referred to as "gentle" words.

Ointment that takes the fever and sting out of a wound is called "gentle."

In one of Plato's works, a child asks the physician to be tender as he treats him. The child uses this term "gentle."

Those who are polite, who have tact and are courteous, and who treat others with dignity and respect are called "gentle" people.

So then, gentleness includes . . . being calm and peaceful when surrounded by a heated atmosphere, emitting a soothing effect on those who may be angry or otherwise beside them-selves, and possessing tact and gracious courtesy that causes others to retain their self-esteem and dignity.[1]

Jesus said, "Come to me . . . for I am gentle" (Matt. 11:28–29). Insecure people think they need to prove their strength or demon-strate their persuasive skill in arguing. Those who are inwardly strong and confident do not need to constantly prove their points. Though at any time Jesus could have demonstrated incredible power, he was gentle. Just as he was approachable, kind, and humble, we are to be so also. We are to have our passions in check, and our disposition should demonstrate softness and touchability. The only way we can do this is to let Jesus help us be like him.

GENTLENESS CAN HELP US FORM BETTER RELATIONSHIPS

You may feel that you simply cannot develop a relationship with certain people. Let's examine how the fruit of gentleness will help you even with difficult people. Possibly the three most challenging groups are those who don't agree with us, those who correct us, and those who let us down.

People Who Always Have a Better Idea or Challenge Our Opinion

When we are around people who seem to constantly disagree with us, we may become defensive, we may turn quiet and unresponsive, or we may give a controlled response. A controlled response is not defensive, nor is it passive. It is a thought-out, rational reply to opposition. There are times when we simply give a calm verbal reply to someone's challenge. Other times the situation lends itself to a very strong but controlled response because it is the only thing that will be effective.

I have always been intrigued with the time "Jesus entered the temple area and drove out all who were buying and selling there" (Matt. 21:12). His statement to the merchants was, "'My house will be called a house of prayer,' but you are making it a 'den of robbers'" (v. 13). Because of the serious nature of the situation, strong action was required. Jesus did not react impulsively; he knew exactly what he was doing.

People were being exploited in the name of religion. Many worshipers were coming into the temple area who sincerely wanted to be obedient in their faith, but merchants were profiting from the people's need for sacrificial animals. This caused great concern to Jesus because it was in direct opposition to God's gracious, generous, and merciful nature. Jesus' response to those who were hypocritical and took advantage of others was calculated and firm (see Matt. 23).

I'm concerned for people who feel exploited today. I have watched people in public ministry sell an item that is supposed to have power to heal or say they will send something to a person in need of healing in exchange for a donation. Innocent, sincere, hurting people respond to these offers thinking that this is what they need to do in order to be healed. Meanwhile, the so-called healers or evangelists rake in money from someone's desperate need. The Bible does give examples of God's using unusual ways to heal people; however, God's gifts, blessings, and grace are not for sale. Too often the church has remained silent in the face of such inappropriate behavior.

People were being distracted from worshiping God.

All the business going on—the noisy, competitive bargaining for prices—made it difficult for people to worship and pray. Although God's temple was to be "a house of prayer for all nations" (Isa. 56:7) and the temple court was the only place Gentiles could go to pray, the court was where the buying and selling were taking place. Those who came to seek God and worship him were quickly distracted and disillusioned by all the noise and lack of reverence.

We need to remember that many who visit our churches today sincerely want to worship God. Do they feel welcome in our church, or do we give them the impression that they are strangers and not really welcome? What do they see and hear when they walk through our church foyer? How do they interpret what goes on before and after the service begins? Do they sense our reverence, sincerity, and love for God? We need to be careful to facilitate a worshipful atmosphere. Irreverent activities, rude behavior, or coldness can turn visitors away.

When Paul wrote to the proud Corinthians, he asked, "What do you prefer? Shall I come to you with a whip, or in love and with a gentle spirit?" (1 Cor. 4:21). When necessary Paul could be confrontational; however, he chose to be gentle as much as possible. He wrote to the Thessalonians, "We were gentle among you, like a mother caring for her little children" (1 Thess. 2:7). When we witness to those who are curious about the gospel, we must be gentle and loving. First Peter 3:15 says, "Always be prepared to give an answer to everyone who asks you to give the reason for the hope that you have. But do this with gentleness and respect." Many times people try to get Christians to argue about their faith, but a gentle and kind yet authoritative answer will often be the thing they remember.

What about those who strongly disagree with us and aggressively try to prove us wrong and make their point at all costs? There is no question that this kind of attack is difficult to handle; thus we must handle it in a mature manner. We can respond in a number of ways. First, we can let the person frighten us and then try to get out of the situation as quickly as possible, avoiding any conversation that would hint of the issue they are so insistent on. Second, we can become just as aggressive and let the adrenaline from our anger push us. Or, third, we can keep our response under control with the fruit of gentleness.

What if it is our teenage child, spouse, employer, neighbor, or friend who frightens us with his or her attack? If we run in fear, we give in to the attacker's wrongful behavior. We must not let fear control us, because if it appears that we have the attitude of "peace at any price," we will never help the person or deal with the situation appropriately. Fear will not only control us in this situation but in other situations throughout life. Instead of running, we may choose to let the attacker know that we will respond later when his or her emotions have cooled down.

If you notice that every time someone disagrees with you, you become defensive and angry, it could mean that you are insecure and feel that you always need to win. When someone disagrees with you and you feel angry, ask yourself, "Why am I angry? What am I afraid of? What do I think I will lose if I give in?" The answer may be that your self-esteem is threatened and you're afraid you will look weak if you let someone else win. There are some things you can do if you are feeling this way. First, when you're angry and you feel that there is a possibility your response may be too aggressive, loud, or hurtful, you can make the decision not to respond at that time. Second, when you are having a disagreement with someone, remember that no one has to win or lose. Rather, finding the truth should be the goal. When truth is determined, the discussion is over. It should make no difference whether you or the other person comes up with the truth.

When gentleness rules our lives, we won't run because we are frightened or respond angrily because we are insecure. Instead, we will be controlled and aware of the proper timing. Proverbs 15:1 tells us, "A gentle answer turns away wrath, but a harsh word stirs up anger." We can choose to respond with a soft, gentle answer or to be just as tough as the person who made the comment. If we are gentle, the tension will likely dissolve. A harsh reply, on the other hand, will be like pouring gasoline on a fire.

James tells us that there is a wisdom that comes from heaven. What does this kind of wisdom look like? It is "first of all pure; then peace-loving, considerate, submissive, full of mercy and good fruit, impartial and sincere" (James 3:17). Then James adds that "peacemakers who sow in peace raise a harvest of righteousness" (v. 18). In other words, if we let the wisdom from heaven guide our actions and reactions, we will be God's peacemakers and will see tremendous results in the way people respond to us in life.

Gentleness chooses the right response. If a strong response is called for, it is thought out, appropriate, and sensitive to the proper timing—strength filled with tenderness.

People Who Correct Us

How do you respond to people who advise you, correct you, or criticize something you have said or done? Next time it happens, listen to yourself and try to evaluate how you feel. One way I sense if persons are mature in the faith and have grown in the area of gentleness is by watching their response when I advise or correct them. Those who are strong in gentleness are not defensive, nor do they become angry. Rather, the opposite happens; they are grateful for the word of correction.

Even when we receive unjustified criticism our response must be guided by gentleness—strength under control. You may feel like snapping back at the one who criticizes you, but instead you must control your feelings and words.

The writer of Proverbs said much about how we receive correction. "Whoever heeds correction is honored" (Prov. 13:18), but "he who hates correction is stupid" (Prov. 12:1). Correction is sometimes difficult to accept, especially when the person giving it uses harsh words or a sharp tone of voice. Nevertheless, correction is necessary in all of our lives, and we would be wise to welcome it.

Countless people journey through life with blind spots, and all of us have them periodically. These are areas of our lives about which very few if anyone can speak to us. Perhaps we are too critical, confrontational, or defensive. Perhaps we don't listen when people speak to us or we tend to gossip or we cannot keep a confidence. These are areas about which we need someone to speak to us in a caring way. If we don't listen to correction, our relationships may be injured and our Christian growth hindered.

We also need to demonstrate gentleness in the way we confront others. The family is the best place to learn and grow in this skill. Husbands and fathers need to be cautious about how they speak to their wives and correct their children. A husband is not to "be harsh" (Col. 3:19) with his wife. Gentleness is to control his response to her and to rule his emotions when he has had a difficult day. Paul instructed fathers, "Do not embitter your children, or they will become discouraged" (Col. 3:21). The way fathers can be sure to prevent pushing their children too hard is to let gentleness rule their words and control their emotions.

Many times I have counseled men who are angry with their boss or about their job or some situation and take it out on their wife and children. This is not an appropriate way to handle our frustrations.

Wives are to have a "gentle and quiet spirit" (1 Peter 3:4). This is a powerful, persuasive attitude that a woman can have. Peter even says that if a woman is married to an unbeliever, he could be "won over" because of her inward beauty. Men are attracted to women who have their emotions and words under control. Most men hate confrontation and will do almost anything to avoid it, such as coming home late, working long hours in the garage, or possibly even getting involved in some destructive behavior. But when a husband senses that peace reigns in the home and that his wife will find ways to encourage him, he is drawn to spend as much time there as possible.

Children are to be obedient to their parents, "for this pleases the Lord" (Col. 3:20). Proverbs 15:5 says, "A fool spurns his father's discipline, but whoever heeds correction shows prudence." Though a parent's rules, discipline, or restrictions may seem out of line, a child's obedience to them will have a tremendous payoff in life. If young people develop a cooperative attitude and learn to control the urge to argue, they will have an edge on others in college and in their chosen career. Gentleness can be part of even small children's lives. Their emotions and verbal responses can be under control as they go through the challenging teenage years and become independent.

To keep peace in the home, we need to "be completely humble and gentle" (Eph. 4:2). Perhaps the most important decision we make—many times each day—is to let gentleness rule our emotions and words.

People Who Let Us Down

When someone has disappointed or failed you, have you been tempted to give that person a piece of your mind? Probably all of us have been there. Paul, however, writes, "If someone is caught in a sin, you who are spiritual should restore him gently" (Gal. 6:1). People will disappoint us from time to time. But remember that you too will sometimes disappoint others.

If we are harsh, pushy, or quick to react, we will repel others and possibly discourage them from trying again. On the other hand, if we are forgiving and encouraging and we try to explain tactfully to them what may have gone wrong and how to avoid the same situation again, we could be the one who will help them succeed.

When Jesus was asked his opinion of what should be done with the woman caught in adultery (the Pharisees wanted to stone her), he protected her and was sensitive to her obvious embarrassment. Though he did not agree with her behavior, he saw the hypocrisy of her accusers and carefully chose a way to respond to their trick question and judgmental attitude. The religious leaders didn't know what to say to Jesus' response, and they and the onlookers walked away. Then Jesus spoke confidentially to the woman about her sin and what she needed to do about it. We can be certain that this woman saw something amazingly different in Jesus' way of addressing her situation.

How do you respond to people who fail or are caught in some kind of sinful behavior? Do you say to yourself, "Ah-ha, I caught them! I *thought* they had problems," and perhaps even gloat over their failure? This is not how God feels about people's sin and failures. Jeremiah wrote, "[God's] compassions never fail. They are new every morning" (Lam. 3:22). And Paul instructed that "we who are strong ought to bear with the failings of the weak" (Rom. 15:1).

How does Jesus correct you when you let him down? Peter

must have felt terribly guilty and ashamed when he lied and said that he was not one of Jesus' disciples (John 18:15–27). But Peter had been afraid. He had watched the soldiers take Jesus, and he didn't want the same thing to happen to him, so he denied the Lord. He failed.

Nevertheless, after Jesus' resurrection, he demonstrated his confidence in Peter by instructing him, "Feed my sheep," which means "Take care of my people." Jesus didn't mention Peter's denial or remind him how much he had let him down. He did the opposite by empowering him to "go for it" and to put the past behind him. Thus Jesus confirmed the words of the psalmist, "[The LORD] will never let the righteous fall" (Ps. 55:22) and "though [a man] stumble, he will not fall" (Ps. 37:24).

Dave Goetz writes in his silhouette of author and pastor Stu Weber,

Growing up, Weber developed a temper, which blossomed in high school and college. "And then I went in the military, " Weber said, "which doesn't do a lot to curb your temper and develop relational skills."

Early in his ministry, he stopped playing church-league basketball altogether; his temper kept flaring, embarrassing himself and the church. A decade passed. "I hadn't had a flash of temper for years," Weber said, "I thought, the Lord has been good. I'm actually growing."

Then his oldest son made the high school varsity basketball squad. "I began living my life again through my son." Weber terrorized the referees. On one occasion seated in the second row, Weber wound up on the floor level, with no recollection of how he got there. He received nasty letters from church members, whom, he says now, "were absolutely right on."

But then he got another note: "Stu, I know your heart. I

know that's not you. I know that you want to live for Christ and his reputation. And I know that's not happened at these ballgames. If it would be helpful to you, I'd come to the games with you and sit beside you."

It was from one of his accountability partners.

"Steve saved my life," Weber said. "It was an invitation, a gracious extension of truth. He assumed the best and believed in me."[2]

When speaking to those who fail us or those whom we have watched fail others, we need to bathe our conversations with gentleness and mercy, As Steve believed in Stu, we can do the same for those around us. Sometimes all a person needs is a nudge of encouragement.

At times I need to bring correction to an employee in the organization I serve. I like to begin the conversation with compliments, then speak to the person as gently as possible. Often I will say, "I know you want to succeed in your program and you have all the abilities and gifts to do it. I'd like to suggest a few things that may help you."

God is merciful (gentle) with us and believes in us. When we fail him he does not reject us but perhaps says something like Steve said to Stu, "I know your heart. I know that's not you. I know that you want to live for Christ and his reputation. . . . If it would be helpful to you, I'll sit beside you."

GENTLENESS CAN HELP US RESPOND IN UNEXPECTED SITUATIONS

I find it interesting to observe how people treat other people. Wayde told me of a recent encounter he had while putting his small bag in the overhead compartment on an airplane. The man sitting below the compartment was intoxicated and said, "If that bag falls on me, I'm going to rip your head off."

Wayde wasn't sure he heard the man correctly or thought perhaps he was trying to be humorous, so he responded by saying, "Excuse me, I didn't understand what you said."

The man then raised his voice and repeated, "I'll rip your head off if your bag falls on me!"

Several rows of passengers in front of and behind the man became quiet as they were surprised by his obnoxious behavior. Wayde briefly looked at him, acknowledging that he heard him, then sat down. (By the way, Wayde mentioned that he felt like responding in kind but decided to keep himself under control and was glad he did.)

We never know how a day may go as we work and live around people. Most days are full of great relationships with people who are trying their best to make their lives work and to get along. Some days, however, we have experiences with people who frighten us with their behavior.

Have you ever been the victim of someone with road rage? Or the recipient of someone's outburst of anger—possibly abuse? How should we respond to such behavior? One thing is for sure: when people are engaging in uncontrolled activity, it is best to let it pass without a response. Let them drive by or say what they're going to say without responding. If you comment back or become angry, it could push them over the edge. If you know them or live with them, you should respond to them when the situation has calmed down. Gentleness will help keep our response under control while we wait for appropriate timing.

All of us have situations in which strangers help us, usually many times each day—the waitress, the airline attendant, the dry cleaner, the gas station attendant, and others. Paul told us how to treat these people: "In humility consider others better than your-selves. Each of you should look not only to your own interests, but also to the interests of others" (Phil. 2:3–4). Thus the best way to make friends and motivate people is to be friendly and sincerely respectful of them as people and for what they do. Be interested in them and remind yourself that they have demands, deadlines, and personal issues of their own. Very likely you will receive better service if you treat others with understanding and gentleness.

Because of my busy travel schedule, I often eat in restaurants. At times I overhear a customer being very rude to a waitress, treat-ing her like something less than human. I can only imagine what the waitress is thinking and what her conversation might be with her peers in the kitchen. Put yourself in her shoes. How would you want to be treated if you were trying to do your best to serve some-one? The golden rule—doing unto others as we would have them do unto us—is always the best way to treat people.

BE STRONG, COURAGEOUS, AND UNDER CONTROL

Jesus spent a tremendous amount of time teaching his disciples. When we read in the book of Acts about the amazing miracles and great evangelistic results the early church experienced, we need to realize that behind these powerful events was a solid foundation of teaching. Jesus was careful to insure that the disciples understood his Beatitudes—"be attitudes"—which contained the truths neces-sary to a successful life. Among them is, "Blessed are the meek, for they will inherit the earth" (Matt. 5:5).

In our power-hungry, aggressive, win-at-any-cost world, "meek" sounds like "weak," and that's the last thing most people want. After all, we need to survive and "get ahead," don't we? Well,

Jesus has the clue to survival. He says, "Learn from me, for I am gentle" (Matt. 11:29). Jesus was anything but weak. He was totally in control of his life, and his self-discipline was extraordinary.

Jesus said, "Learn from me." I want to be like him; do you? Are you willing to let Jesus teach you? If so, he will give you the same teaching he gave his disciples two thousand years ago. Be meek, be gentle, have power under control and a life that demonstrates balance in the way you respond to people.

One of the characteristics of maturity is the ability to listen to wise people. Proverbs 13:10 says, "Pride only breeds quarrels, but wisdom is found in those who take advice." Wise people listen to wise people; they are teachable. God's leaders are open to different opinions and new information. James said, "Humbly accept the word planted in you, which can save you" (1:21). "Humbly" and "gently" come from the same original word as "meekness." "Humbly" means to be teachable, to learn and obey truth.

The godliest people I know listen to the advice of others, are teachable, and are careful in the way they respond to people. Their words are thoughtfully chosen. Some of these people grew up in homes where yelling and fighting to win arguments was the rule. I would expect them to act like those who influenced them, but instead they act like they never lived under those conditions. They are full of wisdom, demonstrate anything but weakness, and are a joy to be around. What happened to them? They connected with the Vine and began producing his fruit of gentleness.

CHAPTER 9

SELF-CONTROL

Mastering Our Passions

The Associated Press recently reported that the president of a Midwestern theological seminary was fired after the trustees determined that his temper had imperiled his leadership. The president confessed to "misappropriation of anger," and "after hours of agonizing discussion and interviews with the president and vice presidents, a majority of the board members concluded that the expressions of anger had irreparably damaged his ability to lead the seminary."[1]

Who would have thought that after years of educational preparation and in-depth study of the Scriptures this president would lose his job because he could not control his emotions.

On the other hand, another article reported that two penniless refugees from Cuba became millionaires because of their ability to *control* their emotions. Humberto and Georgiana came to America in 1960. Humberto learned English in a high school in Long Island, New York; Georgiana spent her early years in Los Angeles. They met when Georgiana was a student at the University of Miami, and they married in 1972. Both eventually landed jobs as reporters for a Fort Lauderdale, Florida, newspaper, a profession that rarely leads to great wealth. However, a math teacher had taught Humberto the importance of compounded interest, and early in the couple's marriage they decided to save every possible dollar for investment.

They bought only small, compact cars and paid their credit card bills in full every month. They shopped at discount stores, clipped coupons, and took sack lunches to work. During some years the couple saved 66 percent of their income. In 1987 they began investing $1,250 a month in five diversified-stock mutual funds. That investment over eight years produced the growth that made them millionaires.[2]

What's the secret to Humberto and Georgiana's success? How could they come from such humble beginnings and achieve so much while the seminary president who had so much quickly lost it? The answer is self-control. If you have it or are willing to get it, many positive things can happen to you. If you don't have it and think you can make it through life without it, you will suffer because of unwise, uncontrolled decisions.

I have had the privilege of officiating in numerous weddings. I have never met a bride or groom who said he or she was looking forward to the possibility of getting a divorce. Yet approximately half of the marriages performed this year will end in divorce. People get divorced for a number of reasons, one of the major reasons being a lack of commitment that originates in couples living together before marriage. Many couples want sexual privileges without commitment. The decision to wait until they are married to have sex is too difficult for many, and the idea of having self-control over one's sexuality while dating is something that is not highly promoted—especially in the television and movie industry. As a result, statistics are now showing that living together before marriage is a major contributor to the tragedy of divorce.

In the National Marriage Project of Rutgers University, Dr. David Popenoe and Barbara Dafoe Whitehead stated that while marriages are held together by "a strong ethic of commitment, cohabiting relationships by their very nature tend to undermine this ethic." The relationship of nonmarried persons differs from married couples in their levels of commitment and autonomy. "Once this low-commitment, high-autonomy pattern of relating becomes learned, it becomes hard to unlearn."

The landmark Rutgers report, *Should We Live Together? What Young Adults Need to Know about Cohabitation Before Marriage*, said, "Living together before marriage increases the risk of breaking up after marriage." It also reported that cohabiting women are twice as likely as married women to be physically abused and are three times as likely to be depressed.

In 1960 only 430,000 couples lived together. That figure increased ten times to 4,236,000 by 1998. Young people see no harm in that trend. Indeed, the report says nearly 60 percent of high school seniors think it is a good idea to live together before getting married.[3] Many of them think, *Why not? It's easier to yield to your urges than to have your desires under control.* But is it really?

WHAT IS SELF-CONTROL?

The Greek word translated "self-control" is a combination of two Greek words: *en kratos. En* means "in" and *kratos* means "strength, power, might, or dominion." A person with *en kratos* is a person who has strength within. *Kratos* is a word that has been passed on to our English language in words like demo*cratic* ("people-power/rule"), theo*cratic* ("God-power/rule"), and auto*cratic* ("self-power/rule").

The question we must ask ourselves is "Who rules our lives?" As we make hundreds of decisions this week and feel emotions throughout each day, who decides what we are going to do and why we will make a decision? Self-control is one of the greatest abilities we can have. However, we must not misunderstand and think that it is our ability that gives us *en kratos*. This fruit develops in our lives as we stay close to Jesus and mature in our Christian walk. Multitudes of people have self-control in one area of their lives but are falling apart in another. Someone has said, "There are men who can command armies but cannot command themselves. There are men who by their burning words can sway vast multitudes but who cannot keep silence under provocation or wrong. The highest mark of nobility is self-control. It is more kingly than regal crown and purple robe."[4]

The ancient Stoics used the term *self-control* to describe a characteristic of a person who was able to morally restrain himself when tempted by evil pleasures, so as to maintain his ethical freedom. In the New Testament it refers to allowing the Holy Spirit to empower a person so that he or she is able to voluntarily abstain from anything (especially immoral sexual passion) that might hinder fulfillment of his or her divinely appointed task.[5]

Self-control is the answer to the question, "How do we keep from yielding to the acts of the sinful nature?" (see Gal. 5:19). Paul comments that the actions of the sinful nature are clear: "sexual immorality, impurity and debauchery; idolatry and witchcraft; hatred, discord, jealousy, fits of rage, selfish ambition, dissensions, factions and envy; drunkenness, orgies, and the like" (vv. 19–21). The list of behaviors may seem extreme, but they certainly are not uncommon in the stories we could read about in today's newspaper. People—yes, even Christian people—can do the things that Paul mentioned. This is one of the reasons he wanted us to understand the difference between yielding to a natural desire and walking in the Spirit. The sinful nature is part of all our lives, and the only way to control it is to live by the Spirit.

We believe that God planned for the list of fruit in Galatians 5:22–23 to begin with love and end with self-control. The ability to have self-control comes as a result of our growing in the preceding eight qualities. The fruit all work together as people experience different situations and temptations in life. No matter what comes our way, whether it is persecution, stress, or a wrong desire, we should handle the situation as Jesus would. He used all of the fruit as he encountered various people and difficult situations.

When we are loving, we are more joyful. When we have love and joy, we have peace. When we have love, joy, and peace, patience is their companion. Kindness will naturally emanate from a disposition of love, joy, peace, patience, and goodness. With these portions of the fruit functioning, a foundation is laid for self-control, which allows us to live a life of balance and gives us the strength to stand against excess.

HOW TO GROW IN SELF CONTROL

In the *Lord of the Rings*, J. R. R. Tolkien described a mysterious and magical ring that possessed great power. Every person who touched the ring became consumed with the desire to own it. But unbeknown to any of them, they had become enslaved by it.

The person who gets entangled in the control of the ring is Frodo. Gandalf warns Frodo that the more the ring is used, the more it will control the user.

"If you had warned me," said Frodo, "or even sent me a message, I would have done away with it."

"Would you? . . . Try!" said Gandalf. "Try now!"

Frodo drew the Ring out of his pocket, again, and looked at it. . . . He had intended to fling it from him into the very hottest part of the fire. But he found now that he could not do so, without great struggle. He weighed the Ring in his hand, hesitating, and forcing himself to remember all that Gandalf had told him; and then with an effort of will he made a movement, as if to cast it away—but he found that he had put it back in his pocket.

Gandalf laughed grimly. "You see? Already you cannot easily let it go, nor will to damage it. And I could not 'make' you—except by force."[6]

Just as the ring enslaved Frodo, pleasures, even seemingly innocent activities and behaviors, can enslave us.

For instance, companies are continually promoting new weight-loss programs. Why? Although food is necessary for life, many people are slaves to food. They do not know how to eat moderately, and they do not know when to stop. Likewise, people become addicted to prescription medication that is intended to help them. People also become addicted to work, sports, television, exercise, sex, and a host of other activities that are not bad if done in moderation and according to God's principles, which are found in the Bible. Without self-control some harmful habit or behavior can control each of us. Proverbs 25:28 says, "Like a city whose walls are broken down is a man who lacks self-control."

GELLING CONTROL OF YOURSELF

Do you feel out of control? If you are the parent of small children, you probably have had times of despair when you wanted to throw your hands up into the air and shout, "I'll never be a great parent!" Remember, God will help you in every aspect of your life. A mother wrote to Dr. James Dobson about a frustrating, out-of-control experience with her child.

Dear Dr. Dobson:

A few months ago, I was making several phone calls in the family room where my three-year-old daughter, Adrianne, and my five-month-old son, Nathan, were playing quietly. Nathan loves Adrianne, who has been learning how to mother him gently since the time of his birth. I suddenly realized that the children were no longer in view. Panic-stricken, I quickly hung up the phone and went looking for them. Down the hall and around the corner, I found the children playing cheerfully in Adrianne's bedroom.

Relieved and upset, I shouted, "Adrianne, you know you are not allowed to carry Nathan! He is too little and you could hurt him if he fell!"

Startled, she answered, "I didn't Mommy."

Knowing he couldn't crawl, I suspiciously demanded, "Well, then, how did he get all the way into your room?"

Confident of my approval for her obedience, she said with a smile, "I rolled him!"

He is still alive and they are still best friends.

Sincerely,

_____ [7]

This letter probably reminds you of a day when you couldn't seem to get anything under control. All of us have had days like that. Part of understanding this fruit in your life is knowing that you can keep trying, keep working at it, and a day will come when you can look back and see your growth. You may also see emotional, physiological, and sociological benefits.

There is a growing body of scientific evidence along with medical studies that confirm that those who attend church regularly and are consistent with their faith are better off both physically and mentally.[8] Though he is not a professing Christian, Harvard professor Herbert Benson admits that humans are "engineered for religious faith." We are "wired for God. . . . Our genetic blueprint has made believing in an Infinite Absolute part of our nature."[9] Consider some of the following findings.

Alcohol abuse

Alcohol abuse is highest among those with little or no religious commitment.[10] One study found that nearly 89 percent of alcoholics said they lost interest in religion during their youth.[11]

Drug abuse

Numerous studies have found an inverse correlation between religious commitment and drug abuse. Among young people, the importance of religion is the single best predictor of substance-abuse patterns. Joseph Califano, former secretary of the Department of Health and Human Services and head of Columbia University's Center on Addiction and Substance Abuse recently released the results of a three-year study showing the relationship between substance abuse and crime. In 80 percent of criminal offenses, alcohol or drugs were implicated.[12] He stated, "Every individual I have met who successfully came off drugs or alcohol has given religion as the key to rehabilitation." Califano now vigorously supports public funding for drug-treatment programs that "provide for spiritual needs."[13]

Depression and stress

Several studies have found that high levels of religious commitment correlate with lower levels of depression and stress.[14] In one Gallup survey, respondents with a strong religious commitment were twice as likely to describe themselves as "very happy."[15] Armand Nicholi, professor of psychiatry at Harvard Medical School and a deeply committed believer, argues from his lifelong experience that Christians are far less likely to experience mental disorders than their secular counterparts. Why? Because "the one essential feature that characterizes all types of depression" is "the feeling of hopelessness and helplessness," and Christians are never without hope.[16]

Suicide

Persons who do not attend church are four times more likely to commit suicide than those who frequently attend. In fact, lack of church attendance correlates more strongly with suicide rates than with any other risk factor, including unemployment.[17]

Family stability

The classic sociological research project "Middletown" studied the inhabitants of a typical American town three times, first in the 1920s and for the third time in the 1980s. The data over this extended period indicated a clear "relationship between family solidarity—family health, if you will—and church affiliation and activity."[18] In a study of the factors that contribute to healthy families, 84 percent of strong families identified religion as an important contributor to their strength. In yet another study, African-American parents cited church influence as significant in rearing their children and providing moral guidelines.[19] A 1978 study found that church attendance predicted marital satisfaction better than any other single variable.[20]

Physical health

Studies have shown that maternity patients and their newborns have fewer medical complications if the mothers have a religious affiliation. Belonging to a religious group can lower blood pressure, relieve stress, and enhance survival after a heart attack. Heart surgery patients with strong religious beliefs are much more likely to survive surgery. Elderly men and women who attend worship services are less depressed and physically healthier than their peers with no religious faith. They are also healthier than those who do not attend worship services but watch religious television at home.[21]

This does not mean that every person who is a Christian is healthy, happy, and successful; however, evidence is convincing that one of the greatest assurances of a fulfilled and in-control life is a relationship with Jesus Christ. Author Patrick Glynn wrote in *God: The Evidence*, "Among the most important determinants of human happiness and well-being are our spiritual beliefs and moral choices."[22] Clinical experience, statistics, and research data make a powerful statement about the typical human condition.

UNDERSTANDING SELF-CONTROL AND DISCIPLINE

Self-control and self-discipline work together. Paul wrote to the Corinthian believers, "Do you not know that in a race all the runners run, but only one gets the prize? Run in such a way as to get the prize. Everyone who competes in the games goes into strict training. They do it to get a crown that will not last; but we do it to get a crown that will last forever" (1 Cor. 9:24–25). Here Paul is giving us a philosophy of life and instruction about how to win in life until we reach the finish line of heaven. He shares several truths.

Life Is a Race

No athlete wins unless he or she is in top condition. The wonderful thing about Christianity is that, because of God's grace, all believers can be in good condition. Paul said, "I can do everything through him who gives me strength" (Phil. 4:13), and this holds true for all of us. Where we may have been out of control before we came to Christ, we now can have self-control because he will give us the ability. Winning life's race requires keeping our lives under control. Proverbs 16:32 tells us, "Better a patient man than a warrior, a man who controls his temper than one who takes a city."

Winning the Race Requires Discipline

Pastor and leader Paul Walker related this personal experience:

> On a cold day back in my football playing days in West Virginia, the field was covered with a mixture of sleet, snow and coal dust. It was not one of the more enjoyable games. I remember coming off the field and thinking to myself, I don't want to go back out there. So I went down to the end of the bench and pulled a parka over my head, trying to hide. The coach took a look at me and said, "What's the matter with you, Walker? It's too soon to quit!" All at once I realized that you never give up.[23]

Discipline is critical in the race of life. Our generation suffers from a lack of determination. We constantly need to discipline our bodies by avoiding activities that would be harmful to them. We must discipline our thinking by being cautious about what we read, watch, or think. We must determine to feed our minds truth and purity. We must discipline our spiritual life by developing habits of Bible study, meditation, fasting, and prayer. Peter said, "Make every effort to add to your faith goodness; and to goodness, knowledge; and to knowledge, self-control" (2 Peter 1:5–6). We not only want to get in shape, but we want to win and not lose.

We Need to Know Where We Are Going

We have all met people who seem to not know where they are going in life. I'm not talking about those who change careers or move from one part of the country to another. I'm talking about *life*. They have not made a commitment to serve Christ and be obedient to his commands. They may attend church sometimes or read their Bibles, but they haven't decided to die to themselves and live for God. In order for them to win the race for eternal life, they need to make up their minds that this is what they want and change directions.

We Need to Know the Value of Reaching the Goal

Jesus said, "I have come that you may have life, and have it to the full" (John 10:10). The prize of eternal life is worth the strict training and denial of our sinful nature. If we keep our eye on the goal and do not let anything distract us, we will understand that it will be worth it all when we get to heaven.

We Cannot Hope to Help Others Be Winners Unless We Are Winners Ourselves

When others watch our life and see us succeeding as we overcome harmful habits, temptations, and behaviors, they will receive encouragement that they can persevere too. They will wonder what makes our lives tick. How do we keep our lives disciplined and our marriages working? How do we avoid destructive habits? Why do we have such an unusual peace in spite of the heartaches of life? When they see us winning life's race, they will wonder where we got all our skills. Our response to them is that they can know the same Jesus we know, and he will enable them to be winners too.

DON'T LOOK BACK

If we are to grow in the area of self-control, we can't let our past mistakes persuade us that we will never live an overcoming life. Some let their failures paralyze them and they quit trying. Perhaps they tried getting a college education but didn't make it; or they had what they thought was a good marriage, but it failed; or they applied for a certain job but were rejected; or they sinned and feel they will never be in relationship with God again. In Christ we can put our past behind us. Paul said, "One thing I do: Forgetting what is behind and straining toward what is ahead, I press on toward the goal" (Phil. 3:13–14).

Florence Chadwick was the first woman to swim the English Channel in both directions. But when she tried to swim from Catalina Island to the California coast, the fog was so thick she could hardly see the boats in her party. She swam more than fifteen hours before she asked to be taken out of the water. Her trainer tried to encourage her to swim on since they were so close to land, but when Florence looked all she saw was fog. So she quit—only one-half mile from her goal. Later she said, "I'm not excusing myself, but if I could have seen the land, I might have made it." Two months after her first attempt she walked off the same beach Into the same channel and swam the distance, setting a new speed record because she could see the land.[24]

If we constantly look back to our failures or the times we didn't accomplish a goal, we will let discouragement come into our lives and won't have the will to try again. We can learn from our mistakes and become better people because we have grown, but we must not let ourselves get stuck in the past.

Many have tried to quit a destructive habit, get their anger under control, or develop a discipline only to fail over and over. As Christians we have an advantage. We can pray, seeking God's forgiveness for sinful behavior and asking him for ways to overcome our habits. We can "forget what is behind" and go after the goal.

YOUR FEELINGS CAN BE IGNORED

Emotions and positive feelings certainly add spice to life, but many people depend on their feelings to determine what kind of day they are going to have or whether they should purchase something they desire. At times, however, feelings can deceive us.

To become more self-controlled we need to be able to rule our feelings. Society constantly bombards us with the idea of following our emotions. Instant credit allows us to purchase whatever we *feel* we need. And because people do not control their spending urges, there are more bankruptcies today than ever before.

Advertisers aim at our emotions. If they can convince our feelings that we need something, there is a good chance we will purchase what they are promoting. Thus television commercials promote new products and new vacation destinations and try to convince us that we need a new car or new entertainment system because the old one doesn't have all the right stuff.

People fall in and out of love, have good and bad days, do healthy and unhealthy activities largely depending on how they feel emotionally. Students decide to study or avoid the books because they feel like they need to watch television or do something else. People avoid work because they emotionally just can't get into it.

Have you ever heard of "blue Monday"? It's the beginning of the work week, school week, or the day one returns from vacation. Because some people don't feel like going back to work after a good weekend off, they may call in sick or drag themselves into their workplace in a bad mood.

British psychiatrist Giles Croft of the University of Leeds determined to discover the legitimacy of the Monday blues. First he divided volunteers into three groups. He gave the first group a report declaring the legitimacy of Monday blues and the second group a report that denied the existence of Monday blues. The third group received nothing to read. Croft found that the first group was more likely to rate Monday as the worst day in the week. He thus concluded that how people expect to feel affects how they do feel.[25]

We may have improper feelings that urge us to do something that is physically, mentally, or spiritually harmful. Temptation feeds on our feelings, and that is where we must win in the battle against sin and behavior that can push our lives out of control. Paul wrote, "The grace of God that brings salvation has appeared to all men. It teaches us to say 'No' to ungodliness and worldly passions, and to live self-controlled, upright and godly lives in this present age" (Titus 2:11–12). This "present age" has a multitude of temptations and attractions that can throw us off course. But God's grace is more powerful than any television commercial, desire, wrong feeling, or temptation. His grace teaches us to say, "No! I will not do that. I don't care how I *feel* about it; I'm going to be self-controlled." We can take charge of our down moods, saying, "I am going to have a good day and rejoice in all that God has done for me." This isn't just positive confession; it is reality. God has done much for all of us.

Another way to control moods and desires is by carefully choosing the company we keep. Paul cautioned, "Bad company corrupts good character" (1 Cor. 15:33). Emotions can be contagious. If we spend a lot of time with those who are emotionally driven rather than rationally driven, we may end up wanting to do what they do. If we have friends who are "mad at the world," we may become like them. Proverbs 22:24–25 warns us, "Do not make friends with a hot-tempered man, do not associate with one easily angered, or you may learn his ways and get yourself ensnared." On the other hand, if we associate with people of good character who are in control of their emotions, they will likely have a good influence on us.

You can choose to overcome your bad moods. Although feelings of temptation, discouragement, and sometimes even depression are common in life, we do not need to let these feelings control us. We can choose to follow Paul's advice: "Whatever is true, whatever is noble, whatever is right, whatever is pure, whatever is lovely, whatever is admirable—if anything is excellent or praiseworthy—think about such things. . . . And the God of peace will be with you" (Phil. 4:8–9).

PERMIT THE HOLY SPIRIT
TO DIRECT YOUR LIFE

The Holy Spirit has everything in control. He has perfect balance and will never operate outside of his boundaries of truth. He knows when anger has gone too far and when fear is not healthy. He knows how much self-discipline we can handle and when we need to relax. With our permission he will grow the fruit of self-control in our lives.

Self-control is not just something we determine to do on our own; it is the fruit of God's presence in our lives. Paul wrote, "Live by the Spirit, and you will not gratify the desires of the sinful nature" (Gal. 5:16).

Living by the Spirit means that we obey the Holy Spirit's instructions on how to live. Theologian Gordon Fee wrote in his book *God's Empowering Presence*, "Spirit people march to a different drummer, and the Spirit empowers them to live in such a way that their lives evidence that fact: their behavior is of a decidedly different character from that of their former way of life. . . . Spirit people, by walking in the Spirit by whom they began life in Christ, will thereby not walk in the ways of their pagan past."[26]

When we live by the Spirit we obey God's Word. We avoid situations and things about which we feel conviction. The Holy Spirit helps us feel sensitive when we get out of balance; then we make the decision to get back into balance. We are careful about what we say, following the instruction of the Holy Spirit. The Holy Spirit who lives in us helps us when we fight battles of temptation, sin, gossip, overeating, discouragement, or anything else. It is not our own effort that allows us to overcome; rather, the Spirit of God helps us get under control and live by the Spirit. Paul wrote to the Philippian believers that "it is God who works in you to will and to act according to his good purpose" (2:13).

WHO HAS CONTROL OF YOUR LIFE?

Carl Linquist wrote in his book *Silent Issues of the Church*,

> Henry Wingblade used to say that Christian personality is hidden deep inside us. It is unseen, like the soup carried in a tureen high over a waiter's head. No one knows what's inside—unless the waiter is bumped and trips!
>
> Just so, people don't know what's inside us until we've been bumped. But if Christ is living inside, what spills out is the fruit of the Spirit.[27]

You may be thinking, *That's true, but what spills out of my life is very different than the fruit of the Spirit.* We sincerely do not want you to go on a guilt trip. We do not want you to feel overwhelmed and frustrated, thinking that there is no way you can get your life together. If you are thinking, *I've tried and tried and tried; I'm not very good at this, so I'm just going to be me and let people take me as I am,* then we encourage you to quit trying to do it on your own, because you can't do it alone. Producing the fruit of self-control is not something that comes naturally; it is supernatural. Therefore, you need God's help.

Permit God to show you his love and mercy. Let him fill you up with himself. Surrender your life completely to Christ and determine that you are going to love him with all of your heart, soul, and mind. As you do this, let him express his attributes through your behavior and in the way you treat people. Focus on him and get so filled up with Christ that he oozes out and impacts everybody with whom you associate. If you're not in the habit of reading the Bible, begin reading the New Testament and ask God to speak to you. Don't try to figure everything out; just be aware of God's personality of love, joy, peace, patience, kindness, goodness, faithfulness, gentleness, and self-control. Underline or memorize the verses that speak of his love for you or of his kindness and mercy toward you.

When you are finished reading, think about what you have read and then find a place to pray. You can pray walking, sitting, lying on the floor, or driving your car. Try to pray about what the Bible has said to you. Be honest with God and admit that it seems impossible to do things his way. Talk to him about your failures and disappointments. He knows you better than you know yourself, and he loves you more than you can imagine. Tell him over and over, "Thank you for your complete forgiveness in my life. Thank you for your love and compassion for me. Thank you for not giving up on me."

Let God take control of your life. When he does you will begin acting like him. You will remind people of Christ as his fruit is supernaturally produced in you.

CHAPTER 10

WINNING THE
BATTLE WITHIN

The Power of a Victorious Life

Some of the finest apples in the world are grown in the beautiful Yakima Valley of Washington State. The fruit is carefully nurtured to the point of excellence. Just driving through the orchards during the early fall makes me hungry.

The Nyberg family has owned one of the orchards in that valley for decades. Like the other fruit farmers, they help supply our kitchen tables with apple products. The bottom line for the Nybergs is to produce quality fruit and as much of it as possible.

I recently telephoned Fred Nyberg and asked him what his secret was for producing such a successful product. He mentioned several things that reminded me of what God does in Christians' lives to help us produce his fruit. Though Nyberg's farm has annually enjoyed an excellent harvest, he spoke of his neighbor, He said,

There is an orchard on the north side of my orchard. Every week the orchardists spray minor elements on the trees as leaf feeds. Those trees have the best of care including the best irrigation system, and the orchard continues to be manicured. Sometimes I wonder how he can afford to continue to spend the money he does. One day I took five minutes to walk through his gala block. His fruit size was huge and the leaf color was of the darkest green. I was envious. As I was admiring his fruit, I thought about how we are to abide in Christ to produce his fruit. My neighbor's trees are drawing life from the same water and the same soil type as mine only a few hundred yards away. My trees are doing well and our nutrition program is good. But he has given his trees the maximum levels of needed nutrition and, as a result, his trees are doing fantastic—not just good.

God is interested in you and me bearing a lot of fruit of the Spirit. Jesus said, "This is to my Father's glory, that you bear much fruit, showing yourselves to be my disciples" (John 15:8).

Three different kinds of fruit are mentioned in the New Testament. One is the kind we eat, another is children, and the third is the spiritual fruit that we have focused on in this book. When we produce fruit that is characteristic of Jesus, the Father is glorified. How can we develop that kind of fruit? Knowing who our enemy is and understanding how committed God is to our growth are key to our fruit bearing.

FARMERS FIGHT THE ELEMENTS; WE FIGHT THE FLESH

Fruit farmers are very aware of the challenges weather can bring in both summer and winter. Depending on the stage of growth, trees can suffer greatly when they experience adverse conditions. Fred Nyberg said,

> Two times in my experience as a nurseryman, in the heart of winter, I have gone through temperatures exceeding twenty degrees below zero for over five days. My nursery and orchard trees were damaged to the point where the tree's ability to draw life from the roots was impaired; or in some of the wood, tissues were destroyed. The tree's ability to draw life was gone. With some of the trees we have cut into the center of the limb and have found them to be dark and partly dead, therefore, unable to pump the needed amounts of water and nutrition up to the leaves and the fruiting limbs. Some of the damage was so severe that we had to destroy the tree, while to save others we cut out the worst limbs. Without the ability to draw life from the soil and water, the tree is of no use.

Just as fruit farmers in the Yakima Valley fight the cold winters, dry summers, and natural elements, we too face a constant battle. If our roots are not deep in Christ, we can be terribly affected by the stress, trials, and temptations of life.

The great struggle within every Christian is between the sinful nature and the Spirit. Paul said, "They are in conflict with each other" (Gal. 5:17). This sinful nature, which will be with us our entire lives, opposes the interests and desires of the Spirit. As a believer in Jesus Christ, however, you have a distinct advantage over your sinful nature. You can choose to live by the Spirit and die to the passions of the flesh. Paul said, "I die every day" (1 Cor. 15:31). A person who yields to the sinful nature may manifest some virtuous characteristics, but the person who lives by the Spirit will manifest all of the fruit of the Spirit.

In Galatians 5:19–21, Paul lists fifteen acts of the sinful nature that can be divided into four categories: *illicit sex* (sexual immorality, impurity, and debauchery), *illicit worship* (idolatry and witchcraft), *breakdown in relationships with people* (hatred, discord, jealousy, fits of rage, selfish ambition, dissensions, factions, envy), and *excesses* (drunkenness and orgies).

Sexual Sins

The first is *sexual immorality* or fornication. This denotes any sexual intercourse outside of marriage. The second, *impurity* or uncleanness, refers to the filthy lifestyle of the person who misuses sex. The third, *debauchery* or licentiousness, describes the activity of the person whose sexual conduct is out of control. Theologian F. F. Bruce comments that a licentious lifestyle "throws off all restraint and flaunts itself, 'unawed by shame or fear' . . . without regard for self-respect, for the rights and feelings of others or for public decency."[1]

Looking at Paul's list of sexual sins, we can't help but think about the day we live in. Sex is big business today, and television producers like to flaunt gratuitous sex to get ratings. Many television programs communicate that sexual intercourse is acceptable outside of marriage. In an atmosphere of less and less restraint, sexual language, behavior, and activity can come into our homes through the Internet, videos, movie channels, sitcoms, dramas, and daytime programming.

Television shows and movies have introduced to the public a plethora of homosexual and lesbian characters and scenarios in the last few years. Watching sitcoms and dramas featuring gay characters has a numbing effect on viewers. That is, each time a person sees immoral behavior, he or she is less shocked and eventually becomes comfortable with it.

The Gay Pride marches in our cities and on our college campuses aren't really celebration times; they are a chance for homosexuals to shake their fists at society and scream, "We don't care what you think! What we do with our sexual life is our business!" While we have compassion for the people involved, it is the flaunting of a sinful lifestyle that is so troubling.

Wrongful Spiritual Experiences

The first wrongful spiritual experience Paul lists in Galatians 5:20 is *idolatry*, which points to any form of worship toward an object, principle, idea, or being other than God. In Colossians 3:5 greed is listed as a form of idolatry, because whatever a person feels greed for can become an object of worship. Second in Paul's list is *witchcraft*, a term that comes from the Greek word *pharmakeia*. Our word *pharmacy* is derived from the same word. In ancient times *pharmakeia* was used to describe two types of behavior: the use of drugs to poison people and, as here, the use of drugs in witchcraft.[2] In Paul's world and in ours today, it is not uncommon for those who are involved in the occult or witchcraft to use drugs to enhance their transcendental spiritual experience. It is also common for those who use illegal drugs to seek some kind of high or spiritual experience outside of Christ.

Wrongful Breakdowns in Personal Relationships

Paul's list of behaviors that will tear apart any marriage, family, church, or friendship is long, perhaps because so much of what we do is wrapped around our relationships with people. The first behavior he mentions is *hatred*. This may refer to hostilities between individuals or between communities on political, racial, or religious grounds.[3] *Discord* or quarrelsomeness looks for opportunities to be disagreeable. Paul is especially concerned about this attitude and behavior disrupting peace in the churches. *Jealousy* or insisting on being number one or overly self-assertive can cause us to resent someone's success, distinction, or recognition when we do not receive the same. *Fits of rage* or explosive anger would include out-of-control anger or outbursts. *Selfish ambition* is the opposite of having a servant attitude. It continually asks, "What's in it for me?" *Dissensions* divide people rather than unite them. Paul instructed the Roman believers to "watch out for those who cause divisions and put obstacles in your way that are contrary to the teaching you have learned" (Rom. 16:17). *Factions* can be viewed as cliques or a sectarian attitude that ignores or turns against those not in one's group. *Envy* is a mean word in the Greek language. It denotes a grudging attitude that cannot bear to even think about someone else's success or prosperity. Socrates said, "The envious are pained by their friends' successes."[4]

These breakdowns in personal relationships can be found throughout our society. We live in a time when many care only about the payoff for themselves, not what they can do for others. Paul wrote, "Mark this: There will be terrible times in the last days. People will be lovers of themselves, lovers of money, boastful, proud, abusive, disobedient to their parents, ungrateful, unholy, without love, unforgiving, slanderous, without self-control, brutal, not lovers of the good, treacherous, rash, conceited, lovers of pleasure rather than lovers of God" (2 Tim. 3:1–4).

A new Shell poll found that Americans feel they are in a "crisis of conscience." The *Washington Times* reported that

> 56 percent of those surveyed said moral problems outrank the environment, the economy and even national defense as America's most serious problem. The worst of these moral woes, according to the poll, are erosion of respect for authority, fellow citizens, and the law; commitment to marriage; personal responsibility of good citizenship; the work ethic; and belief in God and religion. Seventy-two percent said that parents had the most influence on a child's moral and ethical standards, followed by friends, teachers, and clergy.

Sinful Excesses

Paul first lists *drunkenness*, which was a problem in ancient society and most certainly is today. Drunkenness weakens people's rational and moral control. Anything that alters one's ability to think clearly and act responsibly is a problem. Seventy-five percent of all fatal accidents involve drinking by people of all ages. The last word Paul uses is *orgies*—a word frequently used in close association with drunkenness in the New Testament. This is uncontrolled revelry, taking part in unrestrained festivities.

Paul's list is not exhaustive, but it does provide examples of the bad fruit people produce when the Holy Spirit is not in control of their lives. Gordon Fee makes two observations about the activities of the sinful nature in his book *God's Empowering Presence*. First, "The outcome for any individual is predicated on whether or not one is a Spirit person, having become so through faith in Christ Jesus. Thus for Paul, 'inheriting' or 'not inheriting' the kingdom . . . is a matter of whether or not one is a believer."

Fee clarifies that the acts of the sinful nature "do not describe the behavior of believers, but of unbelievers. . . . It is not that believers cannot or never indulge in these sins. It is that 'those who live like this will not inherit the kingdom of God' (Gal. 5:21). Those who live in this way, have no inheritance with God's people. His concern here . . . is to warn believers that they must therefore not live as others who are destined to experience the wrath of God (Col. 3:6)."

Fee's second observation is that "even though Paul is speaking negatively about the destiny of the ungodly, the positive implication of inheriting the kingdom for those who belong to Christ and thus live in the Spirit should not be missed. 'Inheritance' belongs to those who, by the Spirit, give evidence that they are God's rightful 'heirs.'"[5]

You may be thinking, I like that—I'm a Spirit person, but the sinful nature is so strong. I can't seem to get it under control.

How can we control this drive within us? How can we be sure the acts of the sinful nature will not suddenly manifest themselves in our lives? How can we demonstrate to a lost world that Christ truly has made a difference in our character and behavior?

The answer is in knowing that as a born-again Christian, in God's viewpoint and in reality, you have already won the victory over your sin. Paul said, "Those who belong to Christ Jesus have crucified the sinful nature with its passions and desires" (Gal. 5:24). "Have crucified" is past tense. This means that when you gave your life to Christ, your sinful nature, with all of its disgusting behavior, *was* crucified. When Christ was crucified, "he himself bore our sins in his body on the tree, so that we might die to sins and live for righteousness" (1 Peter 2:24). This is why Paul could say,

> We died to sin; how can we live in it any longer? Or don't you know that all of us who were baptized into Christ Jesus were baptized into his death? We were therefore buried with him through baptism into death in order that, just as Christ was raised from the dead through the glory of the Father, we too may live a new life. . . . Count yourselves dead to sin but alive to God in Christ Jesus. (Rom. 6:2–4, 11)

It is a matter of perspective. From God's point of view we are his children. Because of the cross of Christ, our old nature is already dead. From our point of view God administered a fatal dose of the righteousness of Christ to our old sinful nature. That old nature has been given a knockout blow and it is on its way down—it has been crucified. Paul reminded the believers in Colosse, "Once you were alienated from God and were enemies in your minds because of your evil behavior. But now he has reconciled you by Christ's physical body through death to present you holy in his sight, without blemish and free from accusation" (Col. 1:21–22)! From God's view of eternity our cases have already been settled and our names have been recorded in the Lamb's book of life.

A black granite wall called the Vietnam Veteran's Memorial records the names of 58,156 Americans who died in that war. As one looks at the names and observes the reactions of moms and dads, brothers and sisters, sweethearts, or men and women who were part of that war, one's emotions are shaken. Some visitors put small pieces of paper on the wall to trace the name of their family member or friend. Others run their finger over a name, hoping to find some kind of solace or understanding.

For three Vietnam veterans—Robert Bedker, Willard Craig, and Darrall Lausch—a visit to the memorial must be an especially stirring experience. Although their names are on the wall, they are very much alive. Because of a data coding error, they were incorrectly listed as killed in action.

There is no error concerning your name being recorded in God's book of life. The moment yon became a Christian your name was written down. The difference between you and the three men mistakenly written on the Vietnam Memorial is that you are actually dead—to the sinful nature—and you must remind yourself of that.

WE MUST PERMIT OUR CARETAKER TO PRUNE US

Jesus said, "I AM the true vine, and my Father is the gardener. He cuts off every branch in me that bears no fruit, while every branch that does bear fruit he prunes so that it will be even more fruitful" (John 15:1–2). Whether we understand it or not or like it or not, we all need to be pruned—sometimes radically.

My orchard farmer friend explained to me that even in commercial orchards it is difficult to find persons who really understand how pruning affects the trees physiologically. The cause and effect of pruning in dormancy or during the growing season is complex. For example:

- Dormant pruning usually causes vigor in a fruit tree.
- Summer pruning can reduce vigor in a fruit tree.
- Summer pruning before mid-June affects fruit spur development for the next growing season.
- Summer pruning at the right time will enhance the color of the fruit. If pruning is done at the wrong time or too much pruning is done, it will produce sunburn.
- If the farmer doesn't know which limbs have fruit spurs for next year's crop, the inexperienced cutting may reduce the crop for up to two to three years. Pears produce the best fruit on two-to three-year-old wood, so the farmer is always pruning to regenerate fruit wood that is young. Peaches and most soft fruit grow on one-year wood.
- The farmer needs to know how to cut the limbs with no fruit spurs so that fruit spurs develop.
- During the first four to five years of a tree's life, training is critical. Structure limbs are trained or bent at correct angles. If the limb is too flat, it will lose vigor, thus reducing the needed growth and causing the limb to overfruit. If the branch is left too upright, the tree will remain juvenile and will not develop fruit spurs. In many new orchards, trellis systems are used to train and support dwarf trees. This is even more complex.[6]

Wow! I didn't realize all that went into that great apple or peach I frequently enjoy. One thing is very clear to me, however: it is critical that the fruit farmer knows what he is doing. If he doesn't, the end result could be disaster.

As Christians *we* are the branches that need to be pruned. Why? To produce more of the Spirit's fruit. By the way, have you wondered about the branches that are cut off? Fruit farmers call those branches "sucker limbs." They are called that because they suck moisture and nutrients from the tree and give nothing in return. The suckers also produce shade so the sun cannot get to the center of the tree. Since the sun affects how fast the fruit grows and gives it its color, too much shade can have a negative effect on the fruit.

Concerning some people being like useless branches, William Barclay wrote,

Some of [Jesus' followers] are lovely fruit-bearing branches of himself; others are useless because they bear no fruit. Who was Jesus thinking of when he spoke of the fruitless branches? There are two answers. First, he was thinking of the Jews. They were branches of God's vine. Was not that the picture that prophet after prophet had drawn? But they refused to listen to him; they refused to accept him; therefore they were withered and useless branches. Second, he was thinking of something more general. He was thinking of Christians whose Christianity consisted of profession without practice, words without deeds, he was thinking of Christians who were useless branches, all leaves and no fruit. And he was thinking of Christians who became apostates, who heard the message and accepted it and then fell away, becoming traitors to the Master they had once pledged themselves to serve.[7]

Where do you need to be pruned? Have you found a place of rest and trust as God lovingly deals with you in areas that need to be trimmed? Since every Christian needs to be pruned periodically, it is important that we have the right attitude toward God's discipline.

I have always enjoyed the track and field events in the Olympic

Games. Some of the events, such as the relay, are team oriented. In many other events participants are very much alone. Winning or losing largely depends on how well the athletes have disciplined themselves. In his book *Slaying the Dragon*, record holder in the 200- and 400-meter races Michael Johnson, writes,

> Success is found in much smaller portions than most people realize. A hundredth of a second here or sometimes a tenth there can determine the fastest man in the world. At times we live our lives on a paper-thin edge that barely separates greatness from mediocrity and success from failure.
>
> Life is often compared to a marathon, but I think it is more like being a sprinter: long stretches of hard work punctuated by brief moments in which we are given the opportunity to perform at our best.[8]

A Christian's life is something like being a sprinter. We seem to go for weeks without any tension or unusual stress. Then, one day, it not only rains—it pours. Because of our training and discipline, we react in a kingdom way, demonstrating patience and self-control. The sudden difficulty does not throw us off course, because we have been disciplined and trained by the master. We have allowed him to do his work of pruning off what is destructive, unhealthy, and unproductive. Therefore, we are ready for the challenge and will sprint with excellence. Times of discipline, trials, and difficulty can be the most important times of our lives because they build character. Paul wrote, "We also rejoice in our sufferings; because we know that suffering produces perseverance; perseverance, character; and character, hope" (Rom. 5:3–4). Bad times can be our dearest friends, because through these times we can become more focused on who we are in Christ and develop godly behaviors and attitudes that will prepare us for eternity.

On a recent visit to Israel I (Wayde) had the opportunity to view a boat called *The Jesus Boat*, a boat discovered in the Sea of Galilee in 1986 by two brothers. A three-year drought had lowered the water level, and the brothers noticed a partially exposed object covered with mud. As they washed away the caked-on mud, the bow of a fishing vessel appeared. Archaeologists were called to the scene, and they carefully excavated the sunken vessel. They concluded that the brothers had discovered an extraordinary treasure—a fishing boat from Jesus' time. The museum curator proudly described the find. He commented that this boat could have been the boat Jesus used since it was the kind of boat that was used two thousand years ago.

Another pair of brothers also made a discovery that changed their lives. James and John, the sons of Zebedee (nicknamed the "sons of thunder"), were no different than most of us. One day Jesus invited them to become his followers. They wisely accepted his invitation and discovered the most valuable treasure.

What brought about the discovery of *The Jesus Boat*? The three-year drought, which lowered the shoreline in an unprecedented way, allowed the front of the boat to be seen after two millennia.

God's pruning and what may seem like a drought in your life will bring out the best fruit you could imagine. Trusting him as he lovingly trims off the "sucker limbs" is our privilege. He permits times of drought to reveal the true Christlike character in our lives.

WE NEED TO LIVE IN THE SPIRIT TO PRODUCE THE SPIRIT'S FRUIT

"Live by the Spirit, and you will not gratify the desires of the sinful nature" (Gal. 5:16).

As we conclude this book on the fruit of the Spirit, permit

us to give you an assignment. Remind yourself of who you are in Christ. Try to look at yourself from God's perspective. Think about the positive rather than the negative. Instead of focusing on how you are going to wipe out your sinful nature, concentrate on living in the Spirit. Living is a moment by moment process. Focus every day on who you are in Christ and ask him to help you respond to situations and people as he would. Remember, you have God helping you, and as you mature in Christ you will become stronger and stronger in his fruit. You can always trust God to be near when you need his strength. Jeremiah 17:7–8 reminds us of this promise.

> "Blessed is the man who trusts in the LORD,
>> whose confidence is in him.
> He will be like a tree planted by the water
>> that sends out its roots by the stream.
> It does not fear when heat comes;
>> its leaves are always green.
> It has no worries in a year of drought
>> and never fails to bear fruit."

As Christians we have sensitivity to sinful activities and attitudes that those without Christ do not have. Be cognizant of what pulls you down spiritually. It could be a certain type of television program, a friend, or an activity that makes you feel uncomfortable. When this is the case, avoid the source of trouble. You don't need that thing or person in your life, and you do have the ability to say no.

Living by the Spirit means letting your conduct be directed by the Spirit. Gordon Fee explains,

> This appeal to the Galatians, therefore, is just that, an appeal to "go on walking by the very same Spirit by which you came to

faith and with whom God still richly supplies you, including by the working of miracles in your midst." That is, a powerful and experiential—supernatural, if you will—presuppositional base lies behind this imperative . . . Life in the Spirit is not passive submission to the Spirit to do a supernatural work in one's life; rather, it requires conscious effort, so that the indwelling Spirit may accomplish his ends in one's life. One is urged to "walk by the Spirit" or "live by the Spirit" by deliberately "comforming one's life to the Spirit" (v. 25). If such a person is also described as being "led by the Spirit," that does not mean passively; it means to rise up and follow the Spirit by walking in obedience to the Spirit's desire.[9]

WALKING IN THE SPIRIT IS NOT COMPLICATED

We have power to live by the Spirit because he lives in us. Paul reminded the Roman believers, "You are controlled not by the sinful nature but by the Spirit, if the Spirit of God lives in you. And if anyone does not have the Spirit of Christ, he does not belong to Christ" (Rom. 8:9). The Holy Spirit is our constant companion, our ever-present help, and he will encourage us, help us, convict us, and direct our lives. Every Christian has been given an opportunity to live on a completely different level than those without the Holy Spirit. When the Holy Spirit controls our lives we depend on God for everything—every day. Paul continued by saying, "Therefore, brothers, we have an obligation—but it is not to the sinful nature, to live according to it. For if you live according to the sinful nature, you will die; but if by the Spirit you put to death the misdeeds of the body, you will live, because those who are led by the Spirit of God are sons of God" (vv. 12–14).

How do you breathe? You inhale fresh air and exhale bad air.

Automatically, all day long—when you're sleeping, driving your car, taking a walk, working out, or talking with your boss—you are repeating this lifelong habit. Oh, you can stop for maybe two minutes, but after that, it's over.

Living by the Spirit is similar to breathing. We exhale the impure and inhale the pure. We resist and reject the bad (acts of the sinful nature) and embrace the good (fruit of the Spirit). Think of it this way: When you become aware of something you do, think, or feel that is sinful, you deal with it right then. Whatever you're doing, wherever you are, and whoever you're with, you can mentally whisper a prayer and ask God to forgive and help you.

Say you have just said something rude or inappropriate to your spouse or child. You may have overstated something. You feel guilty and wish you hadn't said what you said. When we live by the Spirit we immediately confess our sin and ask for forgiveness. First John 1:9 says, "If we confess our sins, he is faithful and just and will forgive us our sins and purify us from all unrighteousness." When you confess to God that you have spoken inappropriately and pray, "Lord, forgive me for what I said," you are exhaling the sinful act. When you pray, "Lord, help me to control my tongue and to be sensitive to people, especially my family; please help me say words that will bless people and encourage them," you are inhaling the pure.

You may ask, "How often do I need to do this?"

As much as necessary. Whenever you have said something that grieves the Holy Spirit who lives within you, you need to ask God to forgive you, and often you must apologize to the person you hurt. If you have done something sinful, watched something that grieves the Holy Spirit, or had a wrong attitude, you must repeat the process.

You may be thinking, "I'll need to do this all day long."

Then pray and ask for God's help all day long. By doing so

you will develop godly habits. You will become more sensitive to the Holy Spirit in your life and will live by the Spirit. It may seem overwhelming at first. You may need to do it every five minutes. But as you live by the Spirit you will need to "exhale" less often. You may find that you begin having successful days when you live in the power of the Holy Spirit. Or you may have days when you need to be very careful because of what is going on "between your ears." Your thinking may just keep straying in the wrong direction. The important thing is not to allow sin to be in your heart and thus grieve the Holy Spirit. Be careful not to become callused by repressing the Holy Spirit's voice and disobeying him, because this is one of the most dangerous things a person can do in life.

Christians sometimes disobey the Spirit's voice for long periods of time by refusing to change or walk away from the sin in their lives. Paul said, "Be filled with the Spirit" (Eph. 5:18). This is a continuous process. Thus he is saying, "Keep on being filled with the Holy Spirit." The longer we are inhaling him and exhaling sinful activities the deeper our roots will go into the soil of Christian maturity,

As you go through your day, you should endeavor to live by the Spirit. This means that you give him control of your thinking, feelings, and behavior. When you begin to think about acting in a sinful manner, you should immediately speak to God about it. If you are in a crowd and don't want to pray out loud, you can pray silently. God will hear you and help at that moment.

The Bible tells us, "Enoch walked with God; then he was no more, because God took him away" (Gen. 5:24). Think about it. Every day Enoch walked so close to God that a day came when Enoch moved from earth to heaven! Enoch lived by the Spirit throughout each day, and one day, in a blink, he was in heaven.

You can walk with God too—it's a process. Please do not feel that it is impossible for you. The Holy Spirit will help you. You will find yourself becoming more sensitive to people. Your attitude and temper will be affected, and you will begin to notice that you are not as uptight or angry. Listening to certain types of humor and watching certain kinds of television programs will bother you, and you will walk away or turn off the TV. The Holy Spirit will re-direct your life, and you will become more sensitive to him. He will help you act in ways that are holy and righteous. You will find that the more you listen to him, the greater the peace and contentment you will have.

Understand that the battle between the flesh and the Spirit is lifelong. Keep on the lookout for sinful thoughts, temptations, or attitudes, but be optimistic that you will overcome. Resist the flesh and let the Holy Spirit produce his fruit instead.

BEGIN TODAY

While speaking at a retreat center in Cannon Beach, Oregon, I (Wayde) had the opportunity to walk on the beautiful beach and look at Haystack Rock and the huge Pacific Ocean surrounding it. I stood in awe as I watched the largest ocean on the planet break against the sand, rocks, and cliffs of the Oregon coast. I felt small in comparison.

Suppose I wanted to explain the beauty and greatness of this body of water to a group of people in Missouri, where I live, who had never seen an ocean. If I were to fill a five-gallon bucket and take it to them and explain that this is what the ocean looks like, they still could not comprehend the Pacific Ocean. To them it would look like a five-gallon container of salt water. They would not see Haystack Rock or the powerful waves breaking on the beach. They would not be able to see the magnificent coastline and the immense cliffs that drop hundreds of feet into the ocean.

It would be difficult for them to imagine the vastness of the Pacific when looking at the bucket of water.

In like manner, we can't imagine God's vastness, beauty, power, goodness, and love. Paul writes, "For in Christ all the fullness of the Deity lives in bodily form, and you have been given fullness in Christ" (Col. 2:9–10). The "fullness in Christ" is larger than any expanse of water.

You may feel that the fruit of the Spirit is something you desire but is impossible to obtain. You may feel insecure, frightened, and out of step with God's Spirit. Like a tiny container of salt water compared to the Pacific Ocean, you may feel small and insignificant. But remember, "you have been given fullness in Christ." We are not just small containers of God's power and fruit—we are conduits. God fully intends to increase his power and fruit in your life for eternity. If you haven't begun your life in the Spirit, you can begin today.

ACKNOWLEDGMENTS

By the time a book finally reaches the bookstores there are numerous key people involved in the process. These talented people work behind the scenes, and we would like to acknowledge and thank several.

Rosalyn Goodall (Wayde's wife) teaches technical and professional writing and business communication at Southern Missouri State University. She has read, edited, and offered helpful suggestions on every page before it is submitted to the Zondervan team. Her extensive skills and tireless efforts are greatly appreciated. Rosalyn has been a tremendous help on each of our books.

Jack Kuhatschek, senior acquisitions editor for Zondervan, has been a constant encouragement as well as a critical thinker for our writing. His heartfelt opinions, skill, and friendship have been greatly appreciated in the books we have written for Zondervan. We have tremendous respect for Jack and are grateful for his depth of talent.

Laura Weller has been a primary editor for this book. She is a gentle, gifted, and focused editor. She has great skills and knows what a book ought to look like and how it should read. She has offered numerous ideas and suggestions throughout the writing of *The Fruit of the Spirit*. Her counsel was just right on every occasion.

We also want to thank Dr. Stan Gundry, vice president and

editor-in-chief; Joyce Ondersma, manager of author relations; and Sam Hooks, promotions manager, for their efforts on our behalf. We have felt that this book has been a team effort where all have been focused on doing an exemplary job for the glory of God. We are eternally grateful for each one who has assisted us, as we have sincerely desired to encourage Christians to walk in God's incredible Spirit. Only by doing that can we produce His fruit.

NOTES

Introduction

1. Eric Holan, *Colourful Vienna* (Vienna, Austria: Verlag Anton Schroll & Co., 1982), 98.

2. Quoted in George Wool, *Living Fully: Producing Spiritual Fruit* (Lynnwood, WA: Aglow, 1986), 6.

3. Neil Anderson, *Daily in Christ* (Eugene, OR: Harvest House, 1993), June 17.

4. Tamlya Kallaos, "Stewart Gave Faith, Family Top Priority," *Springfield News-Leader,* 31 October 1999, 4A.

5. Ibid.

6. Ibid.

7. Ibid.

8. Ibid., 1A.

9. Ibid., 4A

10. Andrew Murray, "A Life-Union" *Decision* 40, no. 6 (June 1999): 34.

11. Ravi Zacharias, *Deliver Us from Evil* (Dallas: Word, 1996), 82–83.

12. William Barclay, *The Gospel of John* (Philadelphia: Westminster Press, 1976), 2:175.

13. Sid Buzzell, Kenneth Boa, Bill Perkins, *The Leadership Bible* (Grand Rapids: Zondervan, 1998), 1262.

14. Billy Graham, *The Collected Works of Billy Graham* (New York: Inspiration Press, 1993), 497.

15. Martin Luther, *Commentary on Galatians*, Modern-English ed., (Grand Rapids: Revell, 1988), 378.

NOTES

16. Manford George Gutzke, *The Fruit of the Spirit* (Atlanta: The Bible for You, n.d.), 10–11.

17. Quoted in Craig Brian Larson, *Illustrations for Preaching and Teaching from Leadership Journal* (Grand Rapids: Baker, 1993), 125.

18. Peter H. Davids, *The First Epistle of Peter*, New International Commentary (Grand Rapids; Eerdmans, 1990), 193.

19. Graham, *Collected Works*, 497.

20. Richard J. Foster and James Bryan Smith, *Devotional Classics* (San Francisco: HarperSanFrancisco, 1993), 55.

Chapter 1: Love

1. David Ireland with Louis Thrap, *Letters to an Unborn Child* (New York: Harper & Row, 1974), 33–34.

2. Billy Graham, *The Collected Works of Billy Graham* (New York: Inspiration Press, 1993), 506.

3. David Wilkerson, "Keep Yourself in the Love of God," *Times Square Church Pulpit Series*, World Challenge, Inc., P.O. Box 260, Lindale, TX 75771 (25 October 1999), 1.

4. Joseph Stowell, "God's Compassion for Sinners," in *Preaching Today* (Carol Stream, IL: Leadership Resources and Christianity Today Inc.), 4.

5. J. D. Douglas, ed., *The New Bible Dictionary* (London: InterVarsity Fellowship, 1965), 753.

6. Stephen Neill, *The Christian Character* (New York: Association Press, 1955), 21.

7. Quoted in Craig Brian Larson, *Illustrations for Preaching and Teaching from Leadership Journal* (Grand Rapids: Baker, 1993), 126.

8. Stowell, "God's Compassion," 1.

9. Gary Smalley and John Trent, *The Blessing* (Nashville: Thomas Nelson, 1986), 55–58; quoted in Peter Scazzero, *Building Healthy Relationships* (Grand Rapids; Zondervan, 1991), 6.

10. Quoted in Edythe Draper, *Draper's Book of Quotations for the Christian World* (Wheaton, IL: Tyndale, 1992), 219.

11. Quoted in ibid.

12. Quoted in ibid.
13. William Barclay, *The Gospel of John* (Philadelphia: Westminster Press, 1975), 128.
14. Ibid., 129–30.
15. Quoted in Craig Brian Larson, *Choice Contemporary Stories and Illustrations* (Grand Rapids: Baker, 1998), 147.

Chapter 2: Joy

1. Cited in Craig Brian Larson, *Choice Contemporary Stories and Illustrations* (Grand Rapids: Baker, 1998), 114.
2. Stephen Neill, *The Christian Character* (New York: Association Press, 1955), 29.
3. Amy Carmichael, *Gold by Moonlight* (Fort Washington, PA: Christian Literature Crusade, n.d.), 31.
4. Jack Hayford, *Gifts, Fruit and Fullness of the Holy Spirit* (Nashville: Thomas Nelson, 1993), 50.
5. Cited in Larson, *Choice Stories*, 140.
6. Quoted in George Sweeting, *Great Quotes and Illustrations* (Dallas: Word, 1985), 135.
7. Frank B. Minirth and Paul D. Meier, *Happiness Is a Choice* (Grand Rapids: Baker, 1994), 13.
8. C. S. Lewis, *Letters to Malcolm, Chiefly on Prayer* (New York: Harcourt, Brace & World, 1964), 93.
9. William Barclay, *The Letters to the Galatians and Ephesians* (Philadelphia: Westminster Press, 1976), 50.
10. Quoted in Edythe Draper, *Draper's Book of Quotations for the Christian World* (Wheaton, IL: Tyndale, 1992), 359.
11. Ralph Spaulding Cushman, *Hilltop Verses and Prayers* (Nashville: Abingdon-Cokesbury, 1945), 17.
12. Quoted in Sweeting, *Great Quotes*, 260.
13. Quoted in Draper, *Draper's Book of Quotations*, 598.
14. Craig Brian Larson, *Illustrations for Preaching and Teaching from Leadership Journal* (Grand Rapids: Baker, 1993), 266.
15. Malcolm Muggeridge, quoted in Douald McCullough, *Waking*

from the American Dream (Downers Grove, IL: InterVarsity Press, 1988), 145.

16. John Ortberg, *The Life You've Always Wanted* (Grand Rapids: Zondervan, 1997), 72–73.

17. Larson, *Choice Stories*, 101.

18. Quoted in Draper, *Draper's Book of Quotations*, 314.

19. Quoted in ibid., 315.

20. For more in-depth reading on the subject of the baptism in the Holy Spirit, see our book *The Blessing: Experiencing the Power of the Holy Spirit Today* (Grand Rapids: Zondervan, 1998).

21. Quoted in Draper, *Draper's Book of Quotations*, 300.

22. G. K. Chesterton, *Orthodoxy* (Garden City, NY: Doubleday, 1959), 160.

Chapter 3: Peace

1. William Barclay, *The Letters to the Galatians and Ephesians* (Philadelphia: Westminster Press, 1976), 50.

2. Margery Williams, *The Velveteen Rabbit* (New York: Avon Books, 1975), 16–17.

3. Abridged from Paul Harvey Jr., *More of Paul Harvey's The Rest of the Story* (New York: Bantam Books, 1980), 49–50.

4. Found in Jack Kuhatschek, *Peace: Overcoming Anxiety and Conflict* (Grand Rapids: Zondervan, 1991), 10.

5. Adapted from Jacqueline Wasser, "Phobias, Panic, and Fear—Oh My!" *Mademoiselle* 96 (April 1990): 162; cited in Carol Kent, *Tame Your Fears* (Colorado Springs: NavPress, 1993), 42.

6. Corrie ten Boom, *Quotable Quotations*, comp. Albert M. Wells Jr. (Nashville: Thomas Nelson, 1988), 446–47.

7. Charles R. Swindoll and David Lien, *Questions Christians Ask* (Fullerton, CA: Insight for Living, n.d.,), 18; quoted in *Quote Unquote*, comp. Lloyd Cory (Wheaton, IL: Scripture Press, 1977), 378.

8. Henry Drummond, *The Greatest Thing in the World* (Westwood,

NJ: Revell, n.d.); cited in Ada Nicholson Brownell, "Taming your Anger," *The Pentecostal Evangel*, 11 April 1999, 11.

9. Abridged from Brownell, "Taming your Anger," 12–13.

10. Richard Swenson, M .D., is director of the Future Health Study Center in Menomonie, Wisconsin. For more information, see his book *Margin: Creating the Emotional, Physical, Financial, and Time Reserves You Need* (Colorado Springs: Navpress, 1995).

11. Ibid.

12. Philip Edgcumbe Hughes, *Paul's Second Epistle to the Corinthians* (Grand Rapids: Eerdmans, 1962), 135–36.

13. H. Norman Wright, *Crisis Counseling* (Ventura, CA: Gospel Light, 1993), 10.

14. Alexander Solzhenitsyn, *The Gulag Archipelago,* quoted in Philip Yancey, *Where Is God When It Hurts?* (Grand Rapids: Zondervan, 1977), 51.

15. Ira D. Sankey, *My Life and the Story of the Gospel Hymns* (New York: Harper & Brothers, 1906), 168–69.

16. Kuhatschek, *Peace*, 27.

17. Source unknown.

Chapter 4: Patience

1. Jim Cymbala with Dean Merrill, *Fresh Wind, Fresh Fire* (Grand Rapids: Zondervan, 1997), 60.

2. Ibid., 64–65.

3. Gordon Fee, *God's Empowering Presence* (Peabody, MA: Hendrickson, 1994), 449–50.

4. J. I Packer, *Knowing and Doing the Will of God* (Ann Arbor, MI: Servant, 1995), 293.

5. John Ortberg, *The Life You've Always Wanted* (Grand Rapids: Zondervan, 1997), 81–82.

6. Ibid., 82.

7. Associated Press, "Nearly Half of Those Hurt by Violence Knew Assailant," *Chicago Tribune*, 25 August 1997, sec. 1, p. 4.

8. Don Russell, "Road Rage: Driving Ourselves into Early Graves," *Philadelphia Daily News*, July 1997, Local Section, 4.

9. Information courtesy of AAA Foundation for Traffic Safety website, http://www.aaafts.org.

10. Paul D. Meier, Frank B. Minirth, Frank B. Wichern, and Donald E. Ratcliff, *Introduction to Psychology and Counseling* (Grand Rapids: Baker, 1991), 240.

11. William Law, *The Power of the Spirit* (Fort Washington, PA: Christian Literature Crusade, 1971), 124.

12. James C. Dobson, *Parenting Isn't for Cowards* (Waco, TX: Word, 1987), 224.

13. *The Book of Unusual Quotations*, ed. Rudolf Flesch (New York: Harper & Brothers), 1957; quoted in *God's Treasury of Virtues* (Tulsa: Honor Books, 1995), 190.

14. Richard J. Foster and James Byran Smith, *Devotional Classics* (San Francisco: HarperCollins, 1993), 185–86.

15. Lloyd Ogilvie, *Silent Strength for My Life* (Eugene, OR: Harvest House, 1990); quoted in Foster and Smith, *Devotional Classics*, 185–86.

Chapter 5: Kindness

1. Jack Canfield and Mark Victor Hansen, *Chicken Soup for the Soul: A 3rd Serving* (Deerfield Beach, FL: Health Communications, 1996), 237.

2. In Phyllis J. Le Peau, *Kindness: Reaching Out to Others* (Grand Rapids: Zondervan, 1991), 26.

3. *Spirit-Filled Life Bible* (Nashville: Thomas Nelson, 1991), 1,780.

4. William Barclay, *New Testament Words* (Philadelphia: Westminster Press, 1964), 278.

5. Ibid., 279.

6. George Wood, *Living Fully* (Lynnwood, WA: Aglow, 1986), 33.

7. Bonnidell Clouse, *Teaching for Moral Growth* (Wheaton, IL: Victor Rooks, 1993), 148–49.

8. William Barclay, *The Gospel of Luke* (Philadelphia: Westminster Press, 1975), 139.

9. Ibid., 138–39.

10. Jill Briscoe, *Running on Empty* (Wheaton, IL: Harold Shaw, 1995), 20.

11. Quoted in George Sweeting, *Great Quotes and Illustrations* (Dallas: Word, 1985), 159.

Chapter 6: Goodness

1. Claudia Puig, "Crowds Gather to Gawk, Gag at Putrid Plant," *USA Today*, 30 July 1999, 13A.

2. Ibid.

3. *Spirit-Filled Life Bible* (Nashville: Thomas Nelson, 1991), 1,713.

4. Billy Graham, *The Collected Works of Billy Graham* (New York: Inspirational Press, 1993), 518.

5. James Dobson, *Focus on the Family* 22, no. 12 (December 1998), 5.

6. Quoted in George Sweeting, *Great Quotes and Illustrations* (Dallas: Word, 1985), 28.

7. Quoted in ibid.

8. Moira Hodgson, "Lethal Wild Mushrooms Deceive the Unwary," *New York Times*, 22 January 1997, B6.

9. D. James Kennedy, *The Gates of Hell Shall Not Prevail* (Nashville: Thomas Nelson, 1996), 184–85.

10. H. B. London Jr., "Is The Truth Too Much to Handle?" in "The Pastor's Weekly Briefing," *Focus on the Family* 7, no, 20 (14 May 1999): 1. Originally published in *The Washington Post*.

11. H. B. London Jr., "Stats, Stats, Stats," in "The Pastors Weekly Briefing," *Focus on the Family* 7, no. 20 (14 May 1999): 2.

12. Uli Schmetzer, "Wanted Dead or Alive: Manila's Flies, Roaches," *Chicago Tribune*, 17 September 1996, sec. 1, p. 6.

13. The information highway has made home computers the fastest growing and primary mode of distribution of illegal pornography, U.S. Rep. Bob Franks (R-N.J.) stated at a press conference, in introducing the Children's Internet Protection Act, that "an estimated 11 million children have access to the Internet, and more than half of the nation's classrooms currently have access as well.

Donna Rice Hughes of *Kids Online* stated that there are between 72,000 and 100,000 sexually explicit sites on the Internet. Of the approximately 3,900 new sites that go up every day, at least 85 of those sell commercial pornography" (quoted in *Insight*, Family Research Council, Washington, DC).

14. London, "Stats," 1.

15. Roseanne Arnold, *HBO Comedy Hour*, aired June 20, 1992, quoted in *TV, Etc.*, July 1992, 3.

16. Barry Palser and Rachel Scott, "Eternal Impact of a Young life," *The Pentecostal Evangel*, 13 June 1999, 6.

17. Kirk Noonan, "Picking Up the Torch," *The Pentecostal Evangel*, 13 June 1999, 7.

18. Ken Walker, "Blessed Are Those Who Mourn," *Charisma*, September 1999, 44.

19. Ibid., 43–44.

Chapter 7: Faithfulness

1. Philip Yancey, *The Jesus I Never Knew* (Grand Rapids; Zondervan, 1995), 258–59.

2. In David Jeremiah, *God in You* (Sisters, OR: Multnomah, 1998), 83.

3. Max Lucado, *When God Whispers Your Name* (Dallas: Word, 1994), 32–33.

4. Leon Jaroff, "Still Ticking," *Time*, 4 November 1996, 80.

5. *God's Treasury of Virtues*, ed. Honor Books staff (Tulsa: Honor Books, 1996), 323.

6. Quoted in Craig Brian Larson, *Illustrations for Preaching and Teaching from Leadership Journal* (Grand Rapids: Baker, 1993), 197.

Chapter 8: Gentleness

1. Charles R. Swindoll, *Improving Your Serve* (Dallas: Word, 1981), 99–100.

2. Dave Goetz, "Tour of Duty, A Day with Stu Weber," *Leadership*, Spring 1996,

Chapter 9: Self-Control

1. Taken from the Associated Press (name of seminary and president withheld).

2. Randy Fitzgerald, "You Can Make a Million," *Readers Digest*, July 1996, 28.

3. Michael J. McManus, "What Young Adults Need to Know About Cohabitation," *Marriage Savers*, March/April 1999, 3.

4. In Billy Graham, *The Collected Works of Billy Graham* (New York: Inspiration Press, 1993), 527.

5. Jack Hayford, *Gifts, Fruit and Fullness of the Holy Spirit* (Nashville: Thomas Nelson, 1993), 69.

6. J. R. R. Tolkien, *The Fellowship of the Ring* (New York: Ballantine Books, 1965), 93–94.

7. James C. Dobson, *Parenting Isn't for Cowards* (Waco: Word, 1987), 101–2.

8. Following statistics found in Charles Colson and Nancy Pearcey, *How Now Shall We Live* (Wheaton, IL: Tyndale, 1999), 311.

9. Herbert Benson, *Timeless Healing* (New York: Scribner, 1996), 197, 208.

10. D. B. Larson and W. P. Wilson, "Religious Life of Alcoholics," *Southern Medical Journal* 73, no. 6 (June 1980): 723–27.

11. David B. and Susan S. Larson, *The Forgotten Factor in Physical and Mental Health: What Does the Research Show?* (Rockville, MD: National Institute for Healthcare Research, 1992), 68–69.

12. Joseph A. Califano Jr., *Behind Bars: Substance Abuse and America's Prison Population* (New York: The National Center on Addiction and Substance Abuse at Columbia University, 1998), 27.

13. Joseph A. Califano Jr., speech given at the National Press Club, Washington, DC, Jan. 8, 1998.

14. Larson and Larson, *Forgotten Factor*, 76–78.

15. George Gallup Jr., "Religion in America," *Public Perspective*, October/November 1995.

16. Armand Nicholi Jr., "Hope in a Secular Age," in *Finding God at*

Harvard: Spiritual Journeys of Thinking Christians, ed. Kelly K. Monroe (Grand Rapids: Zondervan, 1996), 117.

17. Larson and Larson, *Forgotten Factor*, 76–78.

18. Howard M. Bahr and Bruce A. Chadwick, "Religion and Family in Middletown, USA," *Journal of Marriage and Family* 47 (May 1985): 407–14.

19. See N. Stinnet et al., "A Nationwide Study of Families Who Perceive Themselves as Strong," cited in Patrick Fagan, "Why Religion Matters," *The Heritage Foundation Report* 1064 (25 January 1996): 8; and Velma McBride Murry, "Incidence of First Pregnancy Among Black Adolescent Females Over Three Decades," cited in Patrick Fagan, "Why Religion Matters," *The Heritage Foundation Report* 1064 (25 January 1996): 8.

20. Larson and Larson, *Forgotten Factor*, 73.

21. Ibid., 73–79, 109–23.

22. Patrick Glynn, *God: The Evidence: The Reconciliation of Faith and Reason in a Postsecular World* (Rocklin, CA: Prima, 1997), 67.

23. Paul Walker, *Ministry Now Profiles* 3, no. 7 (March 1999): 1.

24. Abridged from Craig Brian Larson, *Illustrations for Preaching and Teaching from Leadership Journal* (Grand Rapids; Baker, 1993), 96.

25. "Researcher: Monday Funk All in the Mind," *Chicago Tribune*, 2 July 1999, sec. 1, p. 8.

26. Gordon D. Fee, *God's Empowering Presence* (Peabody, MA: Hendrickson, 1994), 433–34.

27. Quoted in Larson, *Illustrations*, 17.

Chapter 10: Winning the Battle Within

1. F. F. Bruce, *The Epistle to the Galatians*, The New International Greek Testament Commentary (Grand Rapids: Eerdmans, 1982), 247.

2. Ibid.

3. Ibid., 248.

4. Ibid., 249.

5. Gordon D. Fee, *God's Empowering Presence* (Peabody, MA: Hendrickson, 1994), 443,

6. Information on fruit farming given by Yakima Valley Nursery, Inc., Yakima, Washington, Fred Nyberg, grower.

7. William Barclay, *The Gospel of John* (Philadelphia: Westminster Press, 1975), 2:174.

8. Michael Johnson, *Slaying the Dragon* (San Francisco: Harper-Collins, 1996), quoted in Craig Brian Larson, *Choice Contemporary Stones and Illustrations* (Grand Rapids: Baker, 1998), 271.

9. Fee, *God's Empowering Presence*, 433.

SCRIPTURE INDEX

Scripture Index